Be Like Tony!   Don't Be Like Chad!

Relationship Leadership
Eddie Mac

© Copyright 2023 | Edward V. McManus | Relationship Media, LLC

Disclaimer

All rights reserved. No part of this book may be reproduced in any form, in whole or in part, except for "fair use" in teaching or research without prior written permission from the author.

The author's intent is only to offer information of a general nature to help you in your quest for Leadership. In the event you use any of the information in this book, the author and the publisher assume no responsibility for your actions.

Although the publisher and the author have made every effort to ensure that the information in this book was correct at press time and while this publication is designed to provide accurate information in regard to the subject matter covered, the publisher and the author assume no responsibility for errors, inaccuracies, omissions, or any other inconsistencies herein and hereby disclaim any liability to any party for any loss, damage, or disruption caused by errors or omissions, whether such errors or omissions result from negligence, accident, or any other cause.

Unless otherwise indicated, all the names, characters, businesses, places, events, and incidents in this book are either the product of the author's imagination or used in a fictitious manner. Any resemblance to actual persons, living or dead, or actual events is purely coincidental.

The publisher and the author make no guarantees concerning the level of success you may experience by following the advice and strategies contained in this book, and you accept the risk that results will differ for everyone. The examples provided in this book may not apply to the average reader and are not intended to represent or guarantee that you will achieve the same or similar results.

The content of this book is not intended to represent any bias or discrimination toward race, ethnicity, religion, sex, age, gender, gender identity, or sexual preference. Any interpretation of such is liability of the reader.

The information presented here does not constitute any psychological or mental health advice. The author is not a psychological professional, mental health provider, or medical practitioner and any interpretation of such is liability of the reader.

ISBN: 978-1-7377405-0-6

Dedication

"Never Fear, Never Weaken."

-Adam McManus

To my son Adam. Thank you for always listening to my advice, trusting me, accepting me for the person I am, and your friendship. My love for you is immeasurable.

Contents

Preface 1
Introduction 7

The Principle of Communication

100% and 100% 17
Us, We, Our 23
Big Pieces and Slow Moving Parts 29
Impact Circle 37
Personalities and Learning 43
Your Reflection 55

The Principle of Respect

You Don't Work for Me 65
"Hey, Look at Me" Syndrome 71
Less Than Perfect 77
Fess Up 85
Work Family Warrior 93

The Principle of Integrity

The First Dance 101
Giving Credit 107
Credibility 117
Why You're the Leader 125
The Second Dance 131

The Principle of Camaraderie

Bridges of Commonality 143
Do Me a Favor 149
I'm in if You're In 155
Power of a Nickname 161
Bump It 167

Bonus 171
Final Words 175
About Eddie Mac 177
I Need Your Help! 179
Training 181
Suggested Next Reads 183
Endnotes 185
References 187

Preface

"A boss has the title, a leader has the people."

-Simon Sinek

As I dismissed the patrol shift with their assignments for the day, roll call was complete and I headed to my office to begin the rest of my day.

While sitting at my desk there was a knock at my door. When I acknowledged his presence, a coworker asked if he could speak with me. As he entered my office and made his way to my desk, I immediately stopped what I was doing, turned to give him my undivided attention, and asked him to have a seat.

This young officer was new to law enforcement and new to our department. I knew he served his country as a United States Marine in the Gulf War and by all accounts was showing to have a promising career ahead of him. So, I was not sure what was coming next. I first thought he might be struggling with a procedural issue, or an equipment issue that needed dealing with at my level. Then again, when a new officer catches you in your office alone there is always the concern that he (or she) wants to talk about quitting.

"What's on your mind?" I asked. As I looked him in the eye he said, "Captain, can I talk to you about something?" I said, "Absolutely!" He told me that when he works for a specific supervisor, he experiences anxiety as soon as he starts getting ready for work. And it gets worse when he gets to work. He said, "The anxiety doesn't exist when you're my supervisor."

At this point I was not sure where the conversation was headed. However, rest assured, he did. The young officer looked at me and said, "I just want you to know that if we were on the battlefield, pinned in a fox hole under heavy machine gun fire, and you told me to take out that machine gun, I'm charging that machine gun." Then, and without skipping a beat, he said, "If that son of a bitch (the other supervisor) ordered me to take out the machine gun, I would refuse his order and accept a court martial." As the conversation ended, I thanked him for his candor, and he thanked me for the way I supervised and treated him. He then left to hit the streets and get to work.

Wow! I was not expecting that! I was a bit shocked by his vigor and blunt statement and this was certainly a compliment. I sat there and began to take inventory of how he might have come to feel the way he did about me versus the supervisor he did not like so much. You see, at our agency each time you are promoted you receive training specific to your rank. The supervisor that the young officer despised so much had the exact training I did. I asked myself, "What is the difference?"

We both had the advanced training of a five-week Executive Development course, an F.B.I. Executive

Development course, a Strategic Leadership course, and at least 100 hours of annual training (mostly Leadership). However, I additionally focused on educating myself about Relationships, personality types, and human behavior. This was during my off time and at my personal expense. I was thirsty to learn how I could have the most impact possible with not only the officers I worked with, but the public as well. I also earned a bachelor's degree in Business Management, giving me insight to organizational and operational dynamics.

It did not take me long to arrive at a conclusion because the answer was as plain as the nose on my face. It was Relationships! My personal desire and effort to forge Relationships with my coworkers was beginning to pay dividends. You see, it is not just about attending a few courses, obtaining a few certifications, getting a college degree, and being in charge. No, it takes a lot of work and a continued desire to build strong Relationships.

This conversation was a catalyst for my yearning to help others become better leaders. It was like throwing gasoline on a fire! Prior to being promoted to the rank of Captain I was a Drug Abuse Resistance Education (D.A.R.E.) officer, Field Training Officer, Commander of our Emergency Response Team (S.W.A.T.), and a Citizen's Police Academy Instructor. Upon my promotion to Captain, I became the administrator of these programs (except the citizen's police academy). As my career continued, I was fortunate enough to hold joint command of our patrol division. This widened my opportunity to build Relationships and help others even more.

Now, let us back up a bit and broaden our view. Having spent my career in the Patrol Division I constantly interacted with people from all walks of life. Most of the time they were in crisis and needed some form of direction (Leadership). I often refer to my career as being a Front-Porch Psychologist (I am not a real psychologist). Every time I made a call I used as many Relationship building and Leadership principles that I could. This enabled me to communicate better with people that sometimes were not easy to communicate with. Then, factor in the emotional energy often present and you have a recipe for things to quickly go south. Did I always accomplish forging a Relationship beneficial to the outcome of the situation? No, of course not, but I tried.

I remember clearing a call and one of my coworkers talking to me as we walked back to our patrol cars. He asked me, "How do you do it?" I curiously said, "Do what?" He said, "You see things we don't. You're able to forecast what's going to happen next, or what someone is going to do next." We talked a bit longer as I explained how I was a student of human behavior, Relationships, and Leadership, and applied my knowledge every time I had the opportunity.

On the academic side of things, I certainly accrued an immense amount of knowledge and training. However, when it comes to real-world application, I could not have been more fortunate than to spend 20 years in law enforcement. It gave me an opportunity to develop my skill set in an environment where I was able to practice continuously. As my career progressed, I took an administrative position. This gave me several opportunities

Preface

to help my coworkers that were specifically in Leadership roles.

Although I retired from law enforcement and no longer in a daily Leadership position, I still have the yearning to help as many people as I can. Yes, I wrote this book because of YOU! I want you to have the tools to succeed as a Leader and I strongly believe that what I have to share will benefit you and your Leadership growth.

I have a close friend that is a physician, and we were talking one day when I asked him about diagnosing patients. I said, "After examining the patient do you form a conclusion of what might be wrong and then run the appropriate test(s) to confirm your diagnosis?" He said, "No, I run tests to prove my diagnosis wrong. If I am unable to prove it wrong, then it is the correct diagnosis. If I prove my diagnosis wrong, then I continue running tests until I find the diagnosis, I cannot prove wrong. Only then will I have the correct diagnosis."

My point is this. I am confident you are reading this book because you want to learn how to be the best Leader possible. So, my challenge is simple. After you have been at it for a while (it takes time), I want you to use the principles from this book and run your own *Relationship Leadership* diagnostic tests. Take an objective look at what you achieved and see if you can prove wrong the *Relationship Leadership* principles you learned in this book. If you are not able to, well, you know the answer....

Introduction

"Leadership is always a matter of Relationships."

-Eddie Mac

Are you new to Leadership? If you are, GREAT! This book was written just for you and is the simplest and most powerful book on Leadership you will ever read! My goal in writing this book is to do everything I can to help you start your Leadership journey with a strong foundation. We are going to work our way through this book together and along the way expect to laugh a little, think a lot, and visualize how the principles learned will help you *Harness the Relationship Leadership Power* to become an awesome leader.

Relationship Leadership is a real world, boots on the ground approach to developing a strong foundation for Leadership. The primary focus is on what you need to be an effective leader and not so much on decision making and tactics. Why, might you ask? The answer is simple, "To be an effective leader you must first have strong Relationships." This is where we will spend our time and energy. You are not going to learn about making battlefield decisions, chasing bad guys, or anything of the like. You are going to learn how relating to your coworkers in certain ways will create desire to follow you. The decisions you make beyond this are up to you. Yes, YOU! Becoming an awesome leader is a journey kind of like walking on shifting sands. As the old saying goes, "The only thing that remains the same is everything changes."

The *Relationship Leadership* principles in this book have all been field tested. They are depicted in various scenarios to illustrate differences in Leadership at the Relationship level. Each scenario is based on a different principal that I experienced or effectively used throughout my career. Included are my mistakes, mistakes I saw others make, and lessons learned.

The Principles

In effort to make this book as simple as possible (my commitment to you) there are four *core Relationship Leadership* principles supported by a collection of *fundamental* principles. This structure will help you easily understand, relate, recall, and use *Relationship Leadership* principles daily!

> **Communication** – Will you follow someone that can't get the message across and won't listen to you?
>
> **Respect** – Will you follow someone that doesn't care about you and doesn't treat you well?
>
> **Integrity** – Will you follow someone that you can't trust, isn't fair, and doesn't always do the right thing?
>
> **Camaraderie** – Will you follow someone that you have no bond with and don't like?

Introduction

Communication
100% and 100%
Us, We, Our
Big Pieces and Slow Moving Parts
Impact Circle
Personalities and Learning
Your Reflection

Respect
You Don't Work for Me
"Hey, Look at Me" Syndrome
Less Than Perfect
Fess Up
Work Family Warrior

Integrity
The First Dance
Giving Credit
Credibility
Why You're the Leader
The Second Dance

Camaraderie
Bridges of Commonality
Do Me a Favor
I'm in if You're In
Power of a Nickname
Bump It

What This Is and What It Is Not

Are you a celebrity, doctor, professional athlete, CEO, famous academic, billionaire, or someone that is in the top one percent of fame and wealth? I am guessing your answer is no, and so is mine! How many books do you think are written with more appeal to status as opposed to real and relatable experience? You see, I spent my whole career being none of these. Instead, I spent time on the front-line building *Relationship Leadership* skills. I am guessing (again) that if you are new to Leadership, you are on the front line as well. Am I right?

"As a leader you are in the Relationship business!" The focus of this book is to show you how Relationships are used to lead others and not cloud your mind with academia, celebrity stories, games won, CEO success, etc. This is a book of short examples from the trenches with enough structure to have a lasting impact on retaining and using what you learn.

Think of it like this. I assume you drive a car, right? Do you know how every part works, what it is made of, how to repair it, and how to diagnose the problem when something isn't right? Probably not, but I bet you know how to put gas in your car, where to put the ignition key, how to start it, put it in drive, and apply the brakes and gas. As the driver you do not need to know all the details of how the car runs, you just need to know how to drive it. This is what you are going to do, learn how to drive the *Relationship Leadership* car. Me? Think of me as the mechanic and this book as your user's manual.

Introduction

Setting the Cornerstone

Do you know much about building a house made of stone? I do not, but I do know the most important thing, the *Cornerstone*. The Cornerstone must be solid, properly placed, and properly anchored. Why? Because the stability of the whole structure depends on the Cornerstone and if it fails everything collapses with it.

Leadership is no different. As I said earlier, "To be an effective leader you must first have strong Relationships." This is your Cornerstone! If not properly placed, you run the risk of your Leadership house collapsing. You are going to learn how to place the Cornerstone so when the sands shift your Leadership house does not have a catastrophic failure! Rebuilding after catastrophic failure is exceedingly difficult and I do not want you to ever have to go down that road.

Meet Tony and Chad

Tony   Chad

These are our main characters, Anthony, and Chadwick. However, in effort to keep it simple we are going to refer to them as *Tony* and *Chad*.

As we move forward these two will be placed in the same scenario(s) and with equal Leadership roles but are not in competition with each other. We are going to learn how effective Tony is at **Harnessing the Power** of *Relationship Leadership* principles and how ineffective Chad is without *Relationship Leadership* principles to guide him.

Tony and Chad work at the Woo-Woo factory, where they make Woo-Woos. Their competitor is the Widget factory, where Widgets are made (you might have heard of them, seems like everyone has worked there). Understand that these two have been working together for about the same amount of time. Also, both earned their Leadership position at the same time, and both completed the same amount of Leadership training mandated by their employer. However, Tony goes the extra mile and continually reads books, studies online, and takes Leadership courses. Chad does not feel he has to do any more than his employer requires. He is the boss and that is good enough for him.

Relationship Leadership Defined

Most authors clarify the direction or theme of their book at the beginning with some sort of literary definition. Instead, I chose to paint you a vivid *Relationship Leadership* picture and let you frame it in the manner that best fits your interpretation. Like I said earlier, "This is the simplest and most powerful Leadership book that you will ever read!"

If you need a definition let us go with *"The development and use of Relationships in a Leadership role."*

Now that you know what *Relationship Leadership* is, we have a Cornerstone to set, Woo-Woos to make, shifting sands to avoid, and *Relationship Leadership Power to Harness!* So, let us put the key in the ignition, start the car, and drive into Chapter1!

The Principle of Communication

Will you follow someone that can't get the message across and won't listen to you?

Chapter 1

100% and 100%

"The roots of effective leadership lie in simple things, one of which is listening. Listening to someone demonstrates respect; it shows that you value their ideas and are willing to hear them."

- **John Baldoni**

Brian stands at Chad's door, takes a deep breath and knocks. Brian is timid by nature and uneasy speaking with strong personality types like Chad.

"Come in," says Chad. As Brian walks into Chad's office, Chad is working at his computer and has music playing. Without looking Chad says, "Have a seat, I will be with you in a minute." He does not turn down the music, nor turn to see who is in his office. Chad is way more interested in accomplishing the task before him than stopping what he is doing to speak with someone.

Brian flinches as Chad's cell phone rings. Almost instantly Chad grabs his cell phone and says, "Hello." A couple sentences into the conversation he swivels his chair away from Brian and with his back now turned to him, Chad leans back into his chair and continues the cell phone conversation. After a few minutes of being totally ignored, Brian eases out of his chair and quietly leaves.

Tony hears a knock at his door and says, "Come in." Brian walks in and asks if he can speak with him about something. Tony immediately says, "Absolutely, have a seat." Tony stops what he is doing, turns his chair to face Brian, places his hands flat on his desk, looks Brian in the eyes and asks, "What's on your mind, Brian?"

Brian went to Tony after attempting to speak with Chad because the Woo-Woo company utilizes a Matrix style of management. Basically, this is where the employees report to more than one leader.[1] Since Tony and Chad have the same level of training and the same Leadership position, employees can report to either.

"I went to Chad's office to talk with him, but he seemed too busy, so I left. I really feel I need to share this information with someone in Leadership, so I came to see you. I discovered something that you may want to look into," says Brian. He then proceeds to tell Tony about the new process he discovered. After speaking with Brian for a while it became obvious that he made a great discovery. Tony tells Brian that he is excited about the new process and is going to meet with the CEO, CFO, and COO to introduce it at the executive level. Tony asks Brian if he will be available to attend the meeting. He smiles big as he replies, "Yes sir!" Tony thanks Brian for his time and tells him he will get back with him as soon as possible with details for the meeting.

The following Monday Brian made his way toward the conference room to attend the meeting with Tony and

Janice (CEO), Marlene (COO), and Archie (CFO). Tony starts the meeting by introducing Brian and explains that Brian discovered a new process while working on the production floor and he invited Brian to share it.

"Well let's hear it," says Janice. Brian stands up, thanks everyone for their time and explains his newly discovered process. When he finishes Janice says, "I like your idea Brian and feel we should explore implementing this new process." Marlene then says, "Brian, as you were speaking, I worked through the production adjustments we will need to make. I don't see any real difficulty in adjusting toward your idea and I think it will increase production by at least 20%, and without an increase in labor." "That is right, I also was crunching numbers while you were speaking, and I don't see any immediate or long-term increase in our costs to make this adjustment. My rough estimate is a bottom-line increase across the board of at least 10%," says Archie. As the meeting ends, everyone thanks Brian for his discovery and encourages him to keep an eye out for more new ideas. Elated, Brian says, "Thank you, I definitely will!"

Two weeks later Tony and Chad are sitting in a special meeting of all company Leadership. Janice opens the meeting and tells everyone, "I called this meeting because of the keen eye of one of our employees, Brian." She explains that Brian discovered a new process for the production floor and met with Tony to discuss it. Tony then contacted her about the discovery, and everyone involved met to discuss the merit of Brian's new process. Janice then says after extensive review by herself, the COO and CFO, Brian's process will be implemented the first day of next month. After answering a few questions from the

Leadership staff Janice adjourns the meeting and Tony and Chad return to their offices.

A couple of hours later Chad walks into Tony's office and says, "You got a minute?" Chad says, "Sure." He stops what he is doing, turns his chair toward Chad, looks him in the eye and says, "What's on your mind?" "When did you learn about Brian's idea?" asks Chad. Tony tells Chad that Brian came to him about a month ago. "I wonder why Brian didn't come to me about his idea?" asks Chad. "He did," says Tony. Chad sternly says, "Bullshit!" Tony tells Chad, "I saw Brian leave your office and come directly to mine and ask to speak with me. One of the first things Brian told me is that he went to speak with you, but you were too busy to speak with him. Chad stands up and says, "Yeah, whatever," as he walks out of Tony's office.

Summary

Well, Chad seemed a bit dismayed, didn't he? What about Brian, huh? Have you ever asked to speak with someone and not receive **100%** of their attention and **100%** of their time? If you have, it is frustrating and disrespectful, isn't it?

Do you remember the young former Marine that came into my office and asked to speak with me? Do you remember the first thing I did when I invited him to have a seat? I stopped what I was doing, looked him in the eye, and gave him 100% of my attention and 100% of my time. What was the first thing Tony did when Brian came into his office? He stopped what he was doing, turned his chair to face Brian, placed his hands flat on his desk, and looked Brian in the eyes.

The point here is when someone asks for your time and attention, YOU give them 100% of your attention and 100% of your time! Stop what you are doing, turn and face them (sitting or standing), look them in the eye, and go from there. If you are too busy and cannot speak with them, ask if it can wait and give them a definite time to follow up. If the phone rings, let it ring or send it to voice mail. If someone walks in, ask them to wait. If you get a text, do not even look at your phone, you can respond later. Why? Because that is what Leaders do!

When you choose to accept the responsibility of Leadership, you make a commitment to your coworkers. If they are asking for your time, it is because there is something they cannot handle on their own. Hence, they need Leadership and if you are going to be an awesome leader, you cannot halfheartedly give your attention and your time! Remember, *100% and 100%!*

Relationship Leadership Power Harnessed
- Respect
- Courtesy
- Attentive
- Importance
- Considerate
- Acknowledgement

Take-Away
Be like Tony and *Don't be like Chad!*

Chapter 2

Us, We, Our

"The leaders who work most effectively, it seems to me, never say "I." And that's not because they have trained themselves not to say "I." They don't think "I." They think "we"; they think "team." They understand their job to be to make the team function. They accept responsibility and don't sidestep it, but "we" gets the credit. This is what creates trust, what enables you to get the task done."

-Peter Drucker

Chad parks in the employee parking lot, locks his car, and strolls across the lot to start his workday. As he walks by the guest parking spots, he notices two of the four spots are taken by cars that he knows belong to employees. This has been going on for quite some time, but not always by the same employees.

Tony hears a knock at the door and says, "Come in." Chad enters and says, "You got a minute?" Tony stops what he is doing, turns toward Chad and says, "Sure, what is on your mind, Chad?" Chad asks Tony if he has noticed employees parking in the guest parking spots. Tony tells him he had not noticed, nor had it been brought to his attention. Chad says, "Well, I've had enough! I'm going to fix this little problem right now!" "By doing what?" asks Tony. "I'm going to send an email to everyone warning not to park in the guest parking spots," says Chad! With a perplexed look on his face Tony replies, "Well, if you feel you must, then have at it." "I will," snips Chad.

Chad sent the following email to all employees:

> *"It has come to my attention that you have been parking in guest parking instead of your designated employee parking. If you continue, I will have your car towed at your expense and you will face disciplinary action. This is your responsibility and I expect you to adhere to this email from this day forward. Contact me if you have any questions."*

Later that afternoon Melanie walks into Tony's office and asks to speak with him. She says, "Why did Chad single me out in his email? His email told me that I was parking in the guest spot, and I never have. Furthermore, he threatened to tow my car for something I didn't do." Tony assures her the email was not directed at her solely and if she is not one of the culprits, she has no worries. "I hope not," says Melanie.

Knock, knock. "Come in," says Tony. Terry walks in and asks Tony why Chad is so spun up about the guest parking? "I feel that he singled me out in his email and threatened towing my car as well," says Terry. Tony assures him he has no worries if he is not the culprit. "I hope not, because all I got out of his email was you, you, you, and it's not me, me, me," exclaims Terry!

Knock, knock. "Come in," says Tony. Jimmy walks in and asks Tony, "What's up Chad's ass today?" Tony calmly says, "Let me guess, the parking email?" "Yep," replies Jimmy. Tony assures Jimmy he has no worries if he is not the culprit. While leaving Jimmy says thanks and, "He better not tow my car!"

For the next week or so no one parked in the guest parking. After that, certain employees began testing the waters a day or two here and there until it became an everyday occurrence again.

Chad storms into Tony's office (without knocking) and asks if he noticed the employee cars parked in guest parking? Tony tells Chad no, since the email he has not paid much attention. Chad is all steamed up and says, "That's it! I'm calling a tow truck for each car in guest parking...right now!" "Calm down, I don't feel there's any need for that just yet. Since I am in Leadership too, how about I send an email addressing the parking issue. Are you okay with that?" asks Tony. Chad takes a deep breath and gives Tony his consent. Then he says, "But I've had enough!"

Tony squares up with his computer monitor and types the following email:

> *"When we have guests at our factory it is usually at our invitation, and we want our guests to have an awesome experience while visiting. Therefore, we*

must be mindful of the simple things that will make their time here as accommodating and memorable as possible. We all share this responsibility and need to be attentive to things such as cleanliness, neatness, and parking for our guests. Remember, our guests are our responsibility."

The next day no one parked in guest parking.

A few weeks later Chad walks into Tony's office and asks him if he noticed that no one has parked in the guests parking for the past six weeks? Tony tells Chad that he did notice. "Also, the place seems a bit cleaner and more tidy than usual. I wonder what changed," says Chad. Tony responds, "I don't know. Maybe it has something to do with the email I sent a few weeks ago addressing cleanliness, neatness, and parking." Chad is instantly miffed that Tony thinks he is the reason for the change. After all, Chad is in Leadership too. He turns and walks away saying, "Yeah, whatever."

Summary

Imagine opening your email and seeing the message from Chad. Would you be upset? Would you feel he was speaking directly at you? I am guessing your answer is yes. If so, why is that?

Now, imagine opening your email and seeing the message from Tony. Would you be upset? Would you feel he was speaking only to you? I am guessing your answer is no. If so, why is that?

Us, We, Our

Communication is crucial to most everything we do in Leadership, especially if we expect to do it well. And email is 100% communication. Chad and Tony could have each spoken the content of their email in a public forum and achieved the same result. So, this really is not about email, it is about effective communication.

When Chad fired his email to his coworkers did you notice what made the content of his message so irritating and confrontational? How about YOU, YOU, YOU! When someone says *you* in person or email, the person on the receiving end hears (sees) YOU! When an email is sent to several people at the same time, the impact is still the same. This opens the door for every individual to interpret the email being directed solely at them. Why? Because YOU is personal and that is how it is perceived.

Let me sum this up for you. Imagine when speaking or sending an email with the word YOU, the other person sees you standing in front of them, arm extended, and your index finger pointing right to the tip of their nose. Remember this image the next time you start to send an email with the word YOU in it, because more than likely this is how it is going to make them feel.

What about Tony's email? What did you notice about the content of his message that made it irritating and confrontational? Nothing! Why is that? What did he say that was so different? First, he never said YOU. His words were carefully chosen to not be offensive and not make his message feel like a personal attack. How did he accomplish this? In place of YOU, Tony used *Us, We, Our.* Rather than bark at everyone about the minor misconduct of a select few, Tony decided to present a solution that everyone could buy into. He created ownership and desire to create company values by including everyone in the solution and treating them equally. This included him as an equal because he said *We* instead of *You.*

Also, did you notice Tony worked cleanliness and neatness into his message? Why? Because this made his message focus less on a single issue (that Chad had everyone spun up about) and gave everyone several things to be mindful of (Issues they can resolve collectively).

ature *Relationship Leadership* Power Harnessed
- Equality
- Inclusion
- Fairness
- Respect
- Teamwork
- Accountability

Take-Away
Be like Tony and *Don't be like Chad!*

Chapter 3

Big Pieces and Slow Moving Parts

"Great leaders are almost always great simplifiers, who can cut through argument, debate and doubt to offer a solution everybody can understand."

-**General Colin Powell**

Tony and Chad are in a meeting with the CEO, Janice. She is explaining to them her expectations of 20% production growth with the implementation of the new procedure Brian recently discovered. They agree that since everyone has been trained, performance should not be an issue. Janice asks Tony and Chad to each come up with an action plan for implementation and then meet with their teams prior to beginning on Monday (the first of the month). She tells them their progress will be monitored for 60 days to see if they are able to meet the production expectation. If so, then Brian's discovery will become the new production procedure for the Woo-Woo factory. Tony and Chad each have a team of 20 coworkers.

Tony starts the meeting with his coworkers and explains to them that, "Beginning Monday we are expected to increase production by 20% using the procedure recently discovered by Brian." He briefly discusses the new training they all received and then gives them simple instructions. While discussing his expectations, Tony creates visual instructions as he is explaining how to implement the procedure. And, because he is speaking to a large group, he keeps his instructions short. Tony tells his team to focus on three goals and in doing so, reaching the increased production should be obtained. "Stay attentive to production time, product flow, and packaging," says Tony. He tells everyone that if there are any issues, they should be brought to Matt's attention. If Matt cannot resolve them then Tony will assist.

Chad starts the meeting with his assigned coworkers and explains to them, "Beginning Monday we are expected to increase production by 20% using the procedure recently discovered by Brian." He briefly discusses the new training they all received and then gives instructions. Chad starts reading from a list he prepared for the meeting. "I want you to listen closely because there are a lot of things you need to pay attention to in order to accomplish your production goal," says Chad. He clears his throat and begins with, "*First,* we need to pay attention to material loading, *second* - electricity usage, *third* -hopper level, *fourth* - distance between product while moving, *fifth* - product weight." This continues for a total of **20** items that Chad expects of them while implementing the new procedure. Chad closes the meeting with instruction to bring all complications, questions, or issues to him.

Chad steps into Tony's office and asks him if he is confident about reaching the 20% production goal in 60 days. Tony

Big Pieces and Slow Moving Parts

proudly says, "Absolutely, we have a great team with awesome talent. I'm greatly confident in their abilities." "What about you?" asks Tony. Chad boastfully responds, "Yep! I gave my team clear instructions of my expectations. They shouldn't have any problems, but if they do, they are to bring them to me and I will find a solution." "Great to hear and good luck, hopefully both teams will succeed," says Tony. Chad stands straight, leans his chest forward just a bit, and while walking away he arrogantly mutters, "I know mine will."

Janice starts the meeting with Tony and Chad following the 60 period. She praises Tony for exceeding the production goal by 5% with a total increase of 25%. Then she turns to Chad and tells him that his team only increased 15%. "How do you explain Tony's team exceeding their goal and your team falling short?" Janice asks. Chad hesitates and then tells her that he is not sure, but he will do better next month. "I hope so. I don't want to have this conversation with you every 30 days," snips Janice. When the meeting ends Tony quickly, and with a big smile on his face, leaves so he can share the news with his team. Chad stands up and while sulking with his held low, slowly walks out of the conference room.

The next day Chad knocks on Tony's door and asks if he can speak with him. Seeing that Chad is still down over yesterday's meeting, Tony asks, "Are you okay?" "I just don't get it," Chad says. "Get what?" Tony inquires. "Why my team didn't reach our goal," responds Chad. "What do you think is the problem?" asks Tony. Chad replies, "I have no clue." Tony tactfully suggests, "Maybe you gave them too many instructions." "No, I was very clear and definitive

Relationship Leadership

with what I expected of them. Hell, I only gave them 20 items of instruction! Plus, I felt confident about our production because I resolved all 30 issues for them," snaps Chad. "How many instructions did you give your team?" Chad asks Tony. "Three," says Tony. "Well how many issues did you resolve?" Chad asks. "Zero because I had to communicate instructions to such a large group, I kept my instruction list short. I also assigned one person to be responsible for problems that may arise. This kept me from being directly involved and potentially hindering their learning by doing it for them," says Tony. Chad sneers at Tony and snips, "Yeah, whatever."

Summary
Location, Location, Location! You have probably heard that before, haven't you? In the real estate business, it is what creates value.

Communication, Communication, Communication, is what creates value in Leadership. If you cannot communicate, you are going to struggle with Leadership.

Let us look at how Chad communicated to his team. He gave them 20 items to focus on while *learning* the new procedure. Not only were they expected to increase production, but they were also dealing with a learning curve at the same time. Do you think that with so many small instructions to focus on and having to learn at the same time was a bit overwhelming? Yeah, me too!

Have you ever seen (or participated in) the demonstration where a large number of people (20 plus) stand in a line and the person at the front of the line whispers a short and

Big Pieces and Slow Moving Parts

simple phrase into the ear of the person next to them? And, then the second person whispers the same phrase into the ear of the third person, and the third to the fourth, and the fourth to the fifth, and so on until the phrase is whispered into the ear of the last person? The last person then repeats what was said to them and it is not even close to what the first person said. A simple phrase by the first person such as, "The sky is blue," will end with the last person saying something like, "It's a cloudy day." What happens is when a person hears the phrase, they interpret it before speaking. But guess what? We all interpret things differently based on our paradigm.

When Chad gave his 20 instructions, how many do you think were absorbed? How did each employee interpret his instructions? How many do you think were incorrectly repeated among his coworkers? What Chad created was a recipe for communication chaos and it showed by his team failing to reach the expected production increase of 20% in 60 days.

What do you think about Chad having to solve 30 issues himself? That is once every two days he helped solve problems with a procedure that was also new to him. Do you feel Chad getting involved on the learning level slowed down his coworker's ability to learn quicker? I do! Why? Because with him being in and out of his team's learning and production, his presence or injection of solutions more than likely only contributed to the chaos. This is because he was not present to see, touch, and feel, (so to speak) how his coworkers were learning so he could understand what led to the problem. Chad was only focused on the fixing the problem and then getting back to his office.

Let us look at how Tony handled these issues. Do you feel only giving his coworkers 3 major goals to achieve was way more effective than Chad's 20 definitive instructions? I do! Why did he do it that way? Tony knew he was communicating to a group and not an individual. Aware of the repeating person to person exercise dynamics we just discussed, he knew he had to keep it simple. So, he came up with only three major goals. This greatly reduced the potential for incorrect interpretation when discussing expectations with each other.

Tony also knew everyone would be learning and if he swooped in to solve the problem and then flew away without being there to see and understand how the problem surfaced, he would only hinder the learning process. Instead, he chose to empower someone for troubleshooting (Matt) that was learning in the same environment and at the same time as the team.

Let us sum this up! Chad created chaos by giving too many directions to a group and then putting himself in position to be in and out of the resolution process. This created a bunch of communication fragments. Going forward, the fragments were not able to sync and create the opportunity for success.

With only 3 major goals given to the group, and with Tony staying out of the way while everyone learned together, his team succeeded.
Look at how many pieces of communication Chad created and how few Tony created. In other words, Tony

succeeded because he communicated using *Big Pieces and Slow Moving Parts.*

Relationship Leadership **Power Harnessed**
- Trust
- Stability
- Empowerment
- Communication
- Teamwork
- Confidence

Take-Away
Be like Tony and *Don't be like Chad!*

Chapter 4

Impact Circle

"Nothing in all the world is more dangerous than sincere ignorance and conscientious stupidity."

-Martin Luther King Jr.

Tony saw Chad go into his office and noticed he was not wearing his normal *better than everyone else* attire. This made him very curious because this is not like Chad. He always makes the effort to dress above and beyond his coworkers, every day!

Tony walks into Chad's office and asks him what is up with his attire for the day? "I decided I'm going to work on the production floor today. I've seen some things that I don't like, and I feel I need to show everyone how it's done," says Chad. "Really? How long has it been since you worked the production line?" asks Tony. "About 15 years, give or take a few months," responds Chad. "You do realize the processes have changed? Also, we upgraded our equipment with the latest technology three times in the past 15 years," says Tony. Chad confidently says, "That doesn't matter, I still have it and they need to see it." "Okay, well good luck and enjoy your day," Tony says, as he walks away shaking his head.

Tony knows that since the time that they were promoted to Leadership, the skill set it takes to work on the production floor has vastly changed and developed into a totally different way of working. Plus, there are two levels of Leadership between Chad and the production workers. The production crew reports to Charlie, Charlie reports to Paula, and Paula reports to Chad. This is beyond Chad's *Impact Circle* and Tony suspects it will not be a good day for Chad and the production crew.

The next day Tony and Chad arrive for work at the same time. As they are walking across the parking lot Tony asks Chad, "How did your day on the production floor go?" Chad sticks his chest out a bit and says, "Awesome! I still have it." "That's good to hear," responds Tony.

A couple of hours into the workday there is a knock at Tony's door. "Come in," says Tony, as he stops what he is doing and turns to face the person knocking. Paula walks in and asks, "Got a minute?" "Sure, what's up?" says Tony. Paula says, "Charlie came to me this morning and told me what a disaster Chad was on the production floor yesterday." "How so?" asks Tony. Paula rants, "Chad screwed up the production line so bad we had to shut down and restart it three times. Also, he broke the hopper intake by overloading it. And he misaligned the print on the packaging, which caused us to unpack several boxes and repack them in correctly printed boxes. Then, when I looked at production at the end of day, we were down 30%!" "Yeah, it does sound like it was a bad day," responds Tony. "It was and I hope we don't have to go through that again. He needs to stay in his office where he belongs,"

Paula says, as she thanks Tony for his time and leaves to finish her workday.

It is lunch time and Tony heads to the cafeteria. As he enters Tony notices Charlie eating by himself. He walks over and asks if he can sit with him? "Sure," says Charlie. "I heard you had an interesting day yesterday," says Tony. "Ha, if you're talking about Chad, it was more like an adventure. Chad is as lost as an Easter egg on the production floor. He screwed up everything he touched and totally wrecked our production numbers for the day. He has no business on the production floor," Charlie strongly says. "That bad, huh?" Tony questions. "Yeah, and the worst of it is that everyone in production, and I mean everyone, is talking about it non-stop. All the production crew views Chad as a total screw up and they're telling everyone that works here," Charlie says to Tony. He takes another bite of his sandwich and as Tony gets up to leave, Charlie stops chewing and says, "Please warn us next time."

Summary
What a mess! Do you think Chad had any business on the production floor doing a job that has drastically changed and he has not done in 15 years? No, me neither.

Should Chad have communicated to Paula what his concerns were and let her handle it? Yes, he should have. He had no business jumping down the Leadership chain, only to feel good about *proving* himself. Chad was clearly outside his *Impact Circle*, and it showed (usually does).

By now you are probably wondering what exactly is an *Impact Circle?* Many experts speak and write about *influence* in the Leadership arena. Although I do not necessarily disagree with them, I have learned that influence can be short lived. It is often used to get someone to perform or act a certain way and may only be for a specific amount of time. Influence may need to happen over and over to keep the ball rolling, so to speak.

Does Impact sound a bit stronger? That is because it is and in Leadership you need to strive to have an Impact in everything you do. People remember the Impact someone or something had on them. This is true in both the positive and negative. As a leader the focus is to always have a positive impact.

Do you think Chad had any positive Impact on the production floor? No, he did not, it was all negative! Everyone in the whole company was talking about him. If there was a company newsletter he would be on the front page and above the fold just as fast as they could print it.

An *Impact Circle* is basically the people that are directly under you in the chain of Leadership. This is where you have the most ability to create positive Impact in Leadership. Then, the level below you should be focused on having the most Impact on the level below them.

Imagine a tower of circles touching each other but not overlapping, one on top of another. Inside your circle are only the people you are directly leading. Inside the circle below yours is the next (lower) level of Leadership leading their people, and so on until you get to the lowest *Impact Circle*. In this case it is the production crew. In other words, Paula reports to Chad (his *Impact Circle*), Charlie reports to Paula (her *Impact Circle*), and the production crew reports to Charlie (his *Impact Circle*).

What usually happens when someone in Leadership gets outside their *Impact Circle* is that potential for skewing the Leadership dynamics of the organization greatly increases. Think of it as a huge ship that begins taking on water, and believe me, I have seen a few ships take on water for being outside their *Impact Circle*. If this is not immediately corrected, the ship begins to sink. Yes, I have also seen a few ships sink, so to speak. Do you think Chad's ship took on water? Yep! Did he sink it? Yep, all the way to the bottom!

By always staying in his *Impact Circle* do you feel Tony harnessed any *Relationship Leadership* power? Sure he did. He never loses credibility with his coworkers because he respects the boundaries, and they only see him in the proper Leadership light. By staying in his *Impact Circle* Tony never creates the opportunity to be perceived any other way. What about Chad? Did he harness any *Relationship Leadership* power by getting outside his *Impact Circle*? No, because he totally wrecked it and now his coworkers will always see him as incompetent.

Relationship Leadership Power Harnessed
- Respect
- Honor
- Considerate
- Adherence
- Credibility
- Approval

Take-Away
Be like Tony and *Don't be like Chad!*

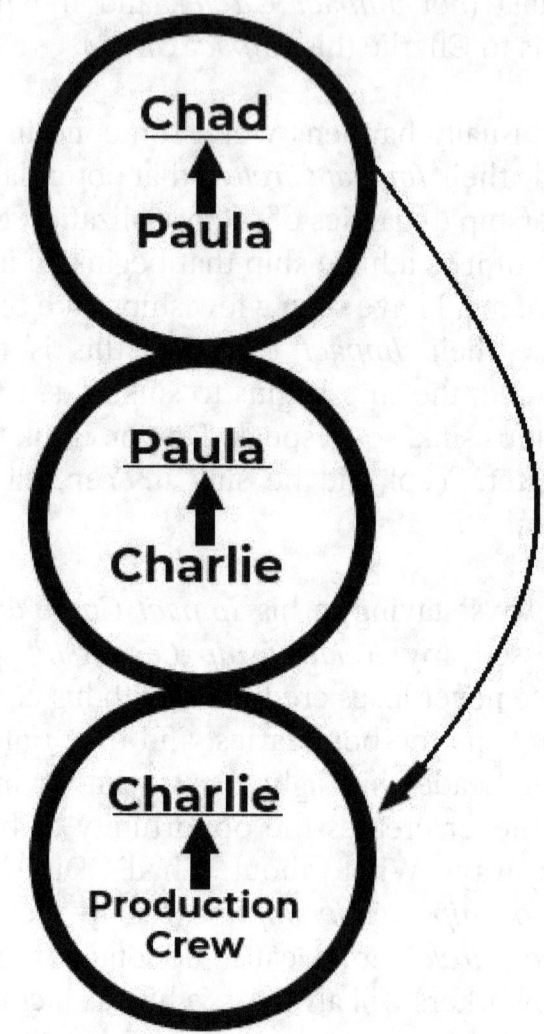

Visual of Chad jumping Impact Circles

Never do this!

CHAPTER 5

Personalities and Learning

"Tell me what you pay attention to and I will tell you who you are."

-José Ortega y Gasset

The holiday season is just around the corner, and it is time for ramping up production at the Woo-Woo factory to meet the upcoming demand. Management anticipates that this will be a record-breaking year for production.

Janice (CEO) begins the meeting with Marlene (COO), Archie (CFO), Tony and Chad. She discusses the anticipated holiday season demand for Woo-Woos', and the production increase needed to meet the demand. Next, Marlene discusses the changes needed in the production processes. Archie then discusses labor, material costs, and margins, with a target of 40% production increase for the months of November and December. After Marlene and Archie finish, Janice asks Tony and Chad if they can meet the holiday production goal. "Yes ma'am," they both answer. "Good to hear! Tony, I want you to meet with each member of your team and go over exactly what is expected of them. Chad, I want you to do the same with your team. Am I clear?" asks Janice. "Yes ma'am," they both say at the same time. "Great! Have a good weekend," says Janice in closing.

Monday morning rolls around and it is time for Tony and Chad to individually meet with their team members. Tony calls Robert into his office and goes over the holiday season production process changes and expected increase. Now, what you need to understand here is that Tony is a student of Personality Types and how to communicate with different ones. He knows Robert has a strong personality and to best communicate with him, Tony gets right to the point. Very succinct and direct communication with Robert and he will get it. Extra information is something that Robert will simply discard and extract only what he needs to get the job done. So, this is what Tony gives him. With Robert, *less is more.*

Tony's next meeting is with Jessica, and she is much different than Robert. Tony knows that Jessica is very detail oriented and logical in her thinking. So, what does he do? Tony gives Jessica every detail of the production process changes and expectations. Naturally, she has questions, and he is prepared for this. Tony answers all of Jessica's questions in detail and to her satisfaction. He knows that she is very analytical, and everything must *fit in the box*, so to speak.

Next meeting is with Mallory. Tony knows she is a bit of a wildcard. He has spent quite a bit of time watching her communicate with coworkers, how she works, how she talks, how she dresses, etc. Tony knows to get through to Mallory he must use a lot of word pictures. She is very visual and creative; it is how she understands and communicates with others. During their meeting he paints several word pictures of the production process changes and expectations. By appealing to her personality type and

Personalities and Learning

learning style, Tony ensures Mallory can *see* what needs to be done. As the meeting closes Mallory says, "Yeah, I can see it, I get it." Tony thinks to himself, mission accomplished.

Chad's first meeting is with Phil. He begins by telling Phil the production process changes and increase for the holiday season. Then, Chad goes through a long list of instructions for Phil to follow. Chad does not understand that this is too much information for Phil's personality type. He overloads him with information, causing Phil to be confused and somewhat unclear of what is expected. Chad is very rigid and not able to be flexible with his communication specific to Phil's personality type and learning style. Much like Robert, all Phil needs is succinct and direct instruction.

Next is Katie. Chad begins by telling Katie the production process changes and expected increase for the holiday season. Then, Chad goes through a long list of instructions for Katie to follow. Much like Jessica this works for Katie. Everything *fits in the box,* and she gets it. Chad got lucky with Katie because his explanation synced with her personality type and learning style.

Chad's last meeting is with Elizabeth. Chad begins by telling Elizabeth the production process changes and expected increase for the holiday season. Then, Chad goes through a long list of instructions for Elizabeth to follow. Again, this is too much information. Elizabeth is dazed and confused. Just like Mallory, she needs to *see* it and she cannot. Chad does not provide any visual explanations, and this is the only way she can absorb and understand what is expected.

It is the end of the holiday season and Janice is pissed! She walks down to Tony and Chad's offices and calls a meeting. "Get to my office right now," she sharply tells them! They both know it is not going to be a good day when, instead of simply calling, the CEO walks downstairs to personally tell you she wants to see you.

Tony and Chad are sitting in Janice's office when she walks in with a file tucked under her arm and a scowl on her face. She slams the folder on her desk, opens it, and removes a spreadsheet. Then she slams the spread sheet on her desk in front of Chad. "Do you care to explain these numbers to me?" she sharply asks Chad. He looks at the spread sheet for a couple of minutes and says, "Ma'am, I don't have an explanation." Janice points to the numbers on the spread sheet that show Chad's holiday season production is up only 10% from normal production. Then she put a spreadsheet in front of Tony and points to his production. Tony's team is up 50% for the holiday season. Janice takes a deep breath, looks at Chad, and with a sternly raised voice says:

> "Chad, because your team only increased 10% during the holiday season, we now have backorders to fill. This is the first time the Woo-Woo factory has not been able to meet holiday season production demand and the first time for backorders. Do you know what this means? I will tell you what it means! It means a lot of people did not get their Woo-Woos for the holiday season and I anticipate this will cause a drop in orders next holiday season! This is not acceptable. Remember when we implemented

Personalities and Learning

> *Brian's new procedure and your team was expected to increase production by 20%, and you only did 15%? Now you have fallen short again! Chad, you have been on the struggle bus for quite some time, and it is time for you to get off the bus. If you cannot, I will stop the bus and throw you off myself! Do you understand what I am telling you? You need to get off at the next stop and figure out how to meet our expectations!"*

Chad hangs his head and quietly mutters, "Yes ma'am, I'll get it figured out. "You really need to," barks Janice. She then turns to Tony and tells him what a great job his team did exceeding the holiday season production goal and to please pass along her congratulations. Tony thanks her and says he will as soon as their meeting is over.

The next morning Chad strolls into Tony's office. "Got a minute?" asks Chad. "Sure, have a seat. What's on your mind?" asks Tony. "I don't understand how your team exceeded holiday production expectations and I fell so short? We were both given the same instructions from Janice and we both met with each team member to explain our holiday production expectations," says Chad.

Tony anticipated that Chad would eventually visit him with questions. And, as usual, he is prepared to help Chad in any way he can. However, he also knows that Chad is not very receptive to instruction or constructive criticism.

Tony tells Chad that his door was open, and he overheard the meetings with each member of his team. He tells Chad that he heard him deliver his expectations the exact same way to each coworker. Tony asks Chad why he did not consider how each person communicates and learns differently? Chad inquisitively responds, "What do you mean?" Tony then explains that he makes the effort to learn each coworker's personality type so he can understand how they learn and communicate. Chad asks Tony what personality types have to do with communication and learning. "Everything," says Tony. "So, you're telling me I need to learn how to identify different personality types and learning styles so I can better communicate with my coworkers when all they have to do is follow my instructions?" snaps Chad. "Yes, that's what I'm telling you! If you want to get off the struggle bus, I will be glad to help you," offers Tony. Chad stomps out of Tony's office muttering, "Yeah, whatever."

Summary

He did it again! Do you remember in Chapter 3 when Chad gave instructions to his team on how to implement the new procedure discovered by Brian? What did he do? He gave detailed and excessive instructions to a group. And he failed to meet his production goals. This time, in a one-on-one environment, he did the exact same thing. Again, total failure! What Chad does not get is how to communicate with people. The style of communication required for each is different.

Do you feel Tony has a handle on how to communicate in a one-on-one environment? Absolutely! He knows that personality type and learning style is different for each person. Tony took this into account and communicated with each person on their level of understanding. He knew a blanket style of communicating would equal total failure.

Personalities and Learning

Tony delivered his message tailored to the individual's personality type and learning style.

As someone new to Leadership, what I need YOU to understand is; this is where the *Relationship rubber meets the Leadership road.* This chapter is a launch pad for your Leadership growth beyond this book. To be a successful leader you will always need to be a student of communication. This hinges on personality types (behavior) and how people learn. We are all unique when it comes to this, and you need to continue your growth in this area every chance you get.

Do you remember earlier in this book when I told you about a coworker asking me how I always seemed to know what people were going to do before it happens, and that I could "see" things others could not? If you recall, my answer was that I am a student of behavior.

When it comes to behavior-based communication what you need to understand is that race, sex, ethnicity, income, social status, education, etc., does not really matter. Why? Because we are all human beings, and we all fall into various categories of predictable behavior and learning styles. There is nothing extra. It is kind of like assembling a bouquet of flowers. There are only so many known flowers on planet earth. So, you might arrange a bouquet of roses, geraniums, and tulips. Then, you might arrange a second bouquet with lilac, lavender, and marigold. Regardless of the chosen flowers, when you are done you have a bouquet of flowers, nothing more. Communicating your message is remarkably similar. You understand what flowers you have to work with (personality types) and pick the correct ones.

Then you arrange them accordingly (based on communication and learning style), and voila! The correct flowers are picked, properly arranged, and you can deliver a beautiful and well received bouquet (message understood).

Now, I am going to dig a little deeper for you because communication at this level is so important and a hinge-pin for your Leadership development. Going forward, the rest will be up to you.

Imagine you and I meet face to face for the first time. If I did not tell you, would you know my Myers-Briggs type is **ENTJ**?[1] Probably not, but if so, what would it tell you about me? What about my Clifton Strengths dominant talent theme being **Strategic Thinking**?[2] Can you recognize it at first sight? Nah, I doubt it. I only chose these two personality assessments to illustrate my point. Which is, as much as I have studied and learned, I still cannot tell a person's Myers-Briggs profile, Clifton Strengths talents, or any other in-depth personality profile at first meeting.

Early in my law enforcement career I recognized that I needed to learn how to quickly identify the differences in people and how to effectively communicate with them, sometimes quickly. In search of this very tool, I was in a local bookstore one day reading the inside cover of books. I just knew it had to be out there somewhere. I picked up an interesting book, read the cover, and Bingo! I found the Holy Grail! Although I was not in Leadership yet, I was in the people business daily and I wanted to know more. I can tell you that what I learned from this book got my ass out of more tight spots as a law enforcement officer than I can remember. I learned how to immediately identify the flowers I needed to pick, how to arrange them, and then properly deliver the bouquet to someone when I initially met them (regardless of the circumstance). As I got better with what I learned, it paved the way for my ascent to Leadership.

The book is titled Psychogeometrics.[3] The more I read, the more it resonated with me. I developed the ability to quickly identify what personality type I was dealing with soon after meeting someone. Just a few observations and maybe a question or two and I was dialed in!

To sum it up, Psychogeometrics places the personality differences of people into five immediately recognizable shapes. This creates a method for easy identification. Left brain hemisphere people are the squares, triangles, and rectangles. Right brain hemisphere people are the circles and squiggles.[4] Once learned, and with uncanny accuracy, when I meet someone, I can quickly identify their shape. Hence, I then know how to communicate with them (make and deliver the bouquet).

What I feel you need to know about learning styles is what I always operate by. There are 3 basic styles, Visual, Audio, and Kinetic. If you do an internet search you will find many different styles, with the percentages of each style often disagreed upon by the experts. So, we are only focusing on these three.

An overwhelming percentage of people learn through visualization. In other words, word pictures. Have you been able to *see* the scenarios unfold and the *Relationship*

Leadership principles appear as we have worked through this book so far? I hope so because I am tapping into your visualization side of learning and communicating. Second to visualization is audio. Connect what people see with what they hear (or read), and you will almost always have your bouquet. Third is kinetic, rarely used, but important to know. A small percentage of people need to "do it" because seeing and hearing does not compute with them. They must touch it, feel it, and work with it to understand.

As for learning styles, remember this is intended to be *the most simple and effective Leadership book you will ever read.* With respect to keeping this commitment I did not get into the weeds with a plethora of research and academic references that will only bog you down. These three learning styles seem to be included in pretty much any book, article, or publication I have read. Mix in the FACT that I have very successfully used these as a guiding light for so many years; *you now know what you need to do to take it to the next level.*

For the record, including Psychogeometrics in this book is not an endorsement. I included it because this is what has worked for me for so many years. If you want to be a great leader (I know you do), it is imperative when you finish reading this book that you research, read, and take courses until you find what gives you the ability to identify personality types and learning styles so you can effectively communicate with your coworkers. It is your bouquet to make, so start picking some flowers!

Relationship Leadership **Power Harnessed**
- Teamwork
- Confidence
- Success
- Achievement
- Communication
- Consistency

Take-Away
Be like Tony and *Don't be like Chad!*

Chapter 6

Your Reflection

"If you would convince a man that he does wrong, do right. But do not care to convince him. Men will believe what they see. Let them see."

-Henry David Thoreau

Tony is walking down the hall and heading to the restroom when he runs into Robert. "Hey Robert," says Tony. Robert stops and with a distressed look on his face says, "Hey Tony, you got a minute?" "Absolutely," responds Tony. Robert asks Tony if he can speak with him about a growing concern he has. It is not just Robert that is concerned; most of the coworkers on Tony's team are having issues. Robert, being an ambassador by nature, feels like he should bring it to Tony's attention.

Janice walks up just about the time Robert starts talking. She says hello and Robert stops talking. Janice says, "Don't let me interrupt, please continue." Being a bit intimidated with the presence of the CEO, Robert is hesitant and looks to Tony for direction. Tony says, "Go ahead Robert, there are no secrets here." Robert then starts telling Tony and Janice that he and several coworkers noticed a shift in the attitude of everyone on Chad's team. He says in the past few weeks most of them are acting a lot like Chad and the collective arrogance is creating friction and conflict between the two teams. "We all work together, but it's becoming more difficult each day," says Robert. Janice rubs her chin and says, "Interesting." Robert continues for a bit more about the growing struggle to communicate and work with Chad's team. Janice excuses herself and heads down the hall toward the restroom.

Jessica walks into the restroom and Janice says hello. She can tell by the look on Jessica's face she is frustrated about something. "What's going on, Jessica, you look frustrated?" inquires Janice. "Well, I am! I probably should let it go and get on with my day but it's really bothering me," says Jessica. Janice asks her what is so frustrating, and Jessica tells her that she just finished a production run with Beverly. "She has become painfully arrogant in the past few weeks. I mean everything is about her. She is difficult to communicate with and acts like she is better at the job than everyone else," Jessica says angrily. She tells Janice that Beverly did not used to be this way. Jessica explains to Janice that Beverly used to be sweet and easy to work with, but since Chad became her leader, it seems like as each day goes by, she becomes more like him. Janice thanks Jessica for sharing and assures her she will investigate the new attitude problem.

Tony is sitting in his office when there is a knock at the door. "Come in," he says. John walks in and asks if he can speak with him for a minute? "Sure, what's on your mind?" asks Tony. John starts by saying that he feels uncomfortable talking about members of Chad's team, but something must give. "How so?" asks Tony. John continues to tell Tony about the growing arrogance of Chad's team members and how it has become difficult to work together. With a look of confusion, John says to Tony, "I was explaining the production procedures to Phil that changed while he was on vacation. When I was done, he looked at me and said 'Yeah, whatever,' and then walked off." He then tells Tony that Chad's team is becoming more like him each day and it is causing problems for everyone on the production floor. Tony thanks him for his time and assures him he will investigate it and get back with him.

A couple of hours later there is another knock at Tony's door. This time it is Mallory. She asks if she can speak with Tony about something. He tells her to have a seat and says, "Let me guess, Chad's team?" "Yes! How did you know?" asks Mallory.

Tony asks what is going on and she says there was a confrontation with Katie over packaging procedures earlier in the day. "She has become so arrogant. We used to be best friends and now I can hardly work with her," Mallory says as she wipes away a tear. Tony tells her he will investigate it and get back with her.

The phone rings and it is Janice. She asks Tony if he can come to her office for a minute. He says he is on his way and hangs up the phone. As Tony shuts his door to go see Janice, he sees Chad shutting his door. "Where are you going?" asks Tony. "Boss wants to see me," says Chad. Tony tells Chad, "Me too." "This should be interesting," Chad mutters, as they both head upstairs to see Janice.

Relationship Leadership

Tony and Chad enter Janice's office and she asks them to have a seat. She starts the meeting by thanking them for their time and the reason she asked to see them. "Something very concerning has come to my attention and I need you to be aware," Janice says sternly. She tells them that she was alerted about a growing sense of arrogance from Chad's team members. Janice continues; she privately spoke with coworkers of both teams, as well as coworkers in other departments, and came to a startling conclusion. Janice tells them her investigation led her to strongly believe that the attitude of Chad's team is quite different than Tony's. Then she unleashes on Chad:

> *"Chad, it seems that everyone not on your team harbors the strong perception that your team members are arrogant. I am talking company wide, not just the production floor. It is causing problems at all levels, and it is not acceptable! Further, the consensus is that your team members were not this way until you became their leader. What in the hell is going on?"*

Chad hangs his head and says, "I don't know, ma'am, but I'll get it corrected." Janice tells Chad that he better because he is starting to wear on her patience, and she is beginning to question if she made the right move when she promoted him into Leadership. "Are you picking up what I'm laying down? Maybe you can learn a thing or two from Tony," snipped Janice.

Janice turns to Tony and tells him that her investigation revealed some interesting facts about his team as well. Tony feels his chest tighten as his shoulders draw in because he has no clue what Janice is talking about. He practices *Relationship Leadership* principles every day with all his coworkers. This includes everyone at the Woo-Woo factory, not just his team. And Tony established and effectively communicated his expectations to all his team members of how they should behave and treat others. Janice sits straight up in her chair and says:

> *"Tony, my investigation revealed what I suspected. Every employee here highly respects you and the members of your team. The consensus is you and your team are always helpful, polite, personable, respectful, courteous, thoughtful, friendly, willing to help, and I can go on, but you get what I am saying. You are doing an excellent job and developing into a great leader. I'm not sure what you are doing but please keep it up, we all benefit!"*

Tony thanks Janice for the kind words and tells her he strives each day to practice *Relationship Leadership* principles. She asks about *Relationship Leadership*, and he gives her a brief explanation. "Hmmm.... maybe we can do some *Relationship Leadership* training for the Leadership team here at the Woo-Woo factory. I know Chad will certainly benefit from a new approach to Leadership," Janice says as she adjourns the meeting.

The next morning Chad walks into Tony's office and asks to speak with him. It was obvious to Tony that Chad is still licking his wounds from their meeting with Janice the afternoon before. He stops what he is doing and gives Chad his undivided attention. Chad begins telling Tony he has no clue why his team has grown into such an uncooperative and arrogant monster. Dreading this was coming, but knowing honesty and integrity are a part of *Relationship Leadership*, Tony swallows hard and asks, "Do you read much?" Chad says he does not like to read that much and asks why? Tony tells Chad, "I am going to share two things that I feel will greatly benefit you." He removes a copy of *Relationship Leadership* from his desk drawer, hands it to Chad, and says follow me.

The two of them get up and walk into Chad's office where there is a large mirror hanging on the wall. Tony says, "I strongly feel there are two answers to what you're dealing with." Chad chuckles and says, "Okay, I get it, I need to read this book." "What is the second answer?" asks Chad. Tony grabs his shoulder and guides Chad to the mirror. He is standing in front of the mirror and confusingly looks at Tony. "Why am I looking at myself in the mirror?" asks Chad. Tony confidently says, "That's your second answer." As he points at Chad in the mirror an immediate scowl comes over his face, Chad is enraged! "You're telling me I'm the problem?" Chad angrily asks. Tony carefully says, "As much as I hate to tell you, yes, I am." Chad's face turns red with anger. He shoves the book into Tony's chest and with a raised voice tells him to keep his stupid Leadership book.

Summary
Well, here we are again! Chad has problems and refuses to entertain the thought that he may be the culprit. He does not understand (and refuses to see) that most problems begin and end with himself. Yes, this goes for you too! If you are having problems, I highly recommend that you spend some time in front of the mirror reflecting on how

Your Reflection

you may have contributed to the problem(s) at hand. It can be an awakening and is a strong Leadership quality.

What do you think is going on here? Well, I will gladly share what I learned (and my thoughts) with you. When Janice praised Tony, did you notice the behavior and perception she described of his team are also exhibited by Tony? Why is that? It is because he is their leader.

When Janice scolded Chad did you notice the behavior and perception she described of his team are also exhibited by Chad? Why is that? Could it be because he is their leader? Hell yes, and you can take that to the bank!

What I want you to understand is that when in Leadership your coworkers will emulate YOU! This may take some time to manifest, but it will happen. And you can take that to the bank as well! Sit back and think about this for a minute. Have you ever wanted to be like someone? If so, why? When you are responsible for leading someone, they look to you for guidance (more about this later in the book). Hence, Leadership! As time goes by relationships develop and they *follow* not only your instruction but your behavior as well! This is evident in the comparison of both teams.

The *Relationship Leadership* Principle I want you to grasp here is that your behavior as a leader makes a direct impact on those that follow you. If you are doing it correctly, they will want to be like you, and they will act like you. As time goes by your reputation as a strong Relationship leader will grow exponentially. Why? Because your direct impact also brings about an *indirect* impact. What indirect impact, you ask? They talk! Do not think for a second your coworkers do not discuss how you treat them, lead them, and generally conduct yourself. Even if they are not under your Leadership, word spreads. And, if your indirect impact is negative, word spreads faster and further!

Have you ever had that one leader everyone knows, always talks positive about, likes, respects, and wants to work for? I have, and more than one. This is where the magic happens and is the crux of this book. YOU can control the magic! Your goal should be when your coworkers look in the mirror, they see YOUR reflection. If not.... maybe it is time to clean the mirror?

Relationship Leadership **Power Harnessed**
- Unity
- Reputation
- Perception
- Respect
- Cooperation
- Cohesiveness

Take-Away
Be like Tony and *Don't be like Chad!*

The Principle of Respect

Will you follow someone that doesn't care about you and doesn't treat you well?

Chapter 7

You Don't Work for Me

"The way a team plays as a whole determines its success."

-Babe Ruth

Today is a big day at the Woo-Woo factory! The research and development team recently discovered technology to create a hybrid product. It is a combination of technology from their competitor, the Widget Factory, with Woo-Woo technology. They are calling it the Widget-Woo.

The Widget-Woo is an awesome new product that both companies believe will greatly benefit their customers. When the Woo-Woo executives approached the Widget executives about their discovery two years ago, both companies agreed to go forward with the project. However, there was the issue of funding. Neither company had excess funds in their budget for the project.

In steps Natalie. She is a wizard at writing grants and locating funding for special projects. She succeeded in securing a State grant for the Widget-Woo project. Therefore, it is a big day. A press release was issued to announce the venture and present will be the governor, lieutenant governor, several state legislators, the mayor, and many local officials. This is a big deal!

Mayor Beasley begins the press conference by giving the background of how the project came to fruition. She explains that the Woo-Woo research and development team discovered the technology, the Widget executives agreed to the partnership, and how the project would not be possible without the State grant.

The research and development team are under the Leadership of Tony and grants are under the Leadership of Chad. After recognizing all public officials present the mayor announces, "At this time, I would like to call Tony to the podium to recognize the research and development team." Tony starts by recognizing the public officials present and thanks them for their interest in the project as well as the executives at both the Widget and Woo-Woo factories. He then says, "At this time I would like to recognize *our* research and development team. Allan is our scientist, Tara is our researcher, and Carol is our engineer." As they all stand in recognition, "I would like to say how proud I am to work *with* this team," says Tony.

Mayor Beasley steps to the podium again and asks Chad to come forward and recognize the grants department. As Chad takes the podium he states, "At this time I would like to recognize Natalie of *my* grants department. She's worked for *me* several years." Natalie stands to be recognized and has an obvious look of disgust on her face. She is pissed! As soon as the meeting is over Natalie quickly retreats to her office.

You Don't Work for Me

A couple of hours later Natalie abruptly walks into Tony's office and asks, "Can we talk?" "Sure," says Tony. "Who in the hell does he think he is? He doesn't sign my paycheck," says Natalie! "Who?" replies Tony. Natalie raises her voice in frustration and says, "Chad!" "I have no clue. You probably need to go next door and ask Chad," Tony says. As she fiercely leaves Tony's office she mutters, "I will, and he better have a damn good answer!"

With a little more vigor and sass, Natalie abruptly enters Chad's office. She walks right up to his desk and loudly says, "Who in the hell do you think you are?" What are you talking about Natalie?" asks Chad. With her bottom lip quivering she says, "At the press conference today you said I worked in *your* grants department, and I worked for *you*." "You do," he replies. "Since when?" asks Natalie. Chad leans back in his chair, interlaces his fingers, and as he cradles the back of his head, confidently says, "The day I was promoted. That's when the grants department became *mine* and *you* started working for *me*." Natalie leans over Chad's desk and says, "You don't sign my paycheck and *I* don't work for *YOU!*" Then she turns and storms out of Chad's office.

Shortly after, Tony walks into Chad's office and asks what Natalie was so spun up about? Chad tells him that she is pissed because during the press conference he referenced the grants department as *his* and her as working for *him*. Tony says, "I agree with Natalie. I do not see research and development as *mine,* nor Allan, Tara, and Carol as *my* employees. We all work together." Chad chuckles and says, "Really? The day I was promoted and became responsible, the grants department became *mine* and all the grants department employees started working for *me*." Tony shakes his head with disbelief and calmly walks out of Chad's office. The next day Natalie quit the Woo-Woo factory and went to work for the Widget factory.

Summary
Wow, what an ass! Chad really has a skewed view of his role. Notice I said, "Role." I made this example somewhat grandiose because you need to understand how powerful of an impact this principle has.

Although all the *Relationship Leadership* principles are important, several hinge from this one. You see, some of the principles are on the personal side and the others on the professional side. This one is on the professional side. What you are learning in this book is how personal and professional work together. As long as they are kept in balance, think of them as a well-oiled machine. If the oil runs dry, then the machine begins to labor and will eventually quit working. In other words, you have to always be personal *and* professional.

Is Natalie, right? I think so! Do you sign the paychecks of those under your Leadership? Unless you own the company or are the CEO, I am going with probably not. I need you to clearly understand how to **ALWAYS** approach this *Relationship Leadership* principle. **YOU** are an employee, the same as everyone else. The only difference is your *role*. Yours is Leadership! So, going forward, show up for work every day with the attitude and focus that you are no more or less important than any other employee. You simply have a different role!

Now, the second part is to **NEVER** introduce a coworker publicly or individually by stating, "Works for me." Instead, refer to them as, "Coworker," or say, "We work together." When referring to anything that collectively includes those under your Leadership **NEVER** say, "Mine," Instead, always refer to as, "Ours."

How do you think Natalie felt when Chad publicly put her below himself? Do you think she felt less important? Of course, she did. Hell, the project would have never happened if she had not secured the funding. And remember, she quit the next day and went to work for the competition.

How do you think Allan, Tara, and Carol felt when Tony publicly addressed himself and them equally? Do you think they felt he was more important to the project's success than they were? Of course not! Their success was equally shared for the news world to see. Oh yeah, and by the way, they did not quit the next day!

Relationship Leadership Power Harnessed
- Fairness
- Respect
- Equality
- Inclusion
- Recognition
- Appreciation

Take-Away
Be like Tony and *Don't be like Chad!*

Chapter 8

"Hey, Look at Me" Syndrome

"Nearly all men can stand adversity, but if you want to test a man's character, give him power."

-Abraham Lincoln

Katie, Jessica, Elizabeth, Robert, and Tony are eating lunch together in the cafeteria when suddenly Katie sees Chad walk in. She lowers her head and quietly mumbles, "Don't look now but King Chad just walked in." Robert says, "Thankfully there are no seats at our table." Then Tony asks, "Why the attitude toward Chad?" Katie tells Tony how self-centered Chad is and how the production crew is growing tired of everything always being about him. "It's nauseating," says Katie.

The conversation continues with everyone at the table discussing Chad's various behaviors. Robert follows with his observation of how Chad makes the effort to look better than everyone else, every day! "It's not a manner of grooming and hygiene, it's the way he presents himself," says Robert. He continues to tell Tony how Chad never has a hair out of place, primps in front of the mirror, and walks around with his nose stuck in the air as if he is better than everyone else. "Hell, I heard he brings a shirt to work every day and changes halfway through the shift, so he stays looking better than all of us," Robert proclaims.

Katie chimes in and says, "Yeah, with all the company achievement patches on his shirt Chad looks like a professional race car driver." (All employees wear the same uniform shirt, and the company gives award patches to be displayed on the shirt, but it is optional.)

Elizabeth pipes up and says, "Have you ever paused to look at all the photos in his office? None of them are friends or family photos, they are all of Chad accomplishing something or winning an award.

Jessica takes her turn, "Yeah, Chad has so many plaques, awards, and framed certificates on his office wall that you can't tell what color the wall is. He even has scouting awards from his childhood and high school sports trophies displayed for all to see. It's like a shrine for all that enter his office to hail King Chad."

Katie can't resist a second shot at Chad, "Oh, and that damn mirror hanging on his wall. It is bad enough to have the mirror, but full length? He is without a doubt a legend in his own mind!"

Everyone breaks from lunch and heads back to work. Tony is a little perplexed with the growing animosity toward Chad, but he is not Chad's supervisor. He decides to let it ride for a bit to see if the attitude toward Chad improves. Although Tony knows that Chad often has problems with Leadership simply because he cannot get out of his own way, he is hopeful for improvement.

"Hey, Look at Me" Syndrome

Knock, knock! It is Mallory asking Tony if she can speak with him. Tony invites Mallory in and asks her what he can do for her. She explains a problem with production that she is struggling with and asks for his advice. After a brief discussion about best options, Mallory thanks Tony for his input and heads back to work.

Knock, knock! It is Beverly asking Tony if she can speak with him. Tony invites Beverly in and asks her what he can do for her. She explains that she is having some difficulty dealing with a coworker and asks his advice on how to deal with the issue. After discussing options and giving Mallory some encouragement, she thanks Tony for his time and heads back to work.

Knock, knock! It is Rick asking Tony if he can speak with him. Tony invites Rick in and asks what he can do for him. Rick has been out on extended sick leave and wants to go over recent changes in the production process (Brian's idea) that were implemented while he was out. When they finish Rick looks at Tony and says, "I just want to thank you for the way you lead us. It is so intimidating to be around Chad and to be in his office. Being around you is extremely comfortable, and your office is so inviting. There's no shrine, you don't out dress me, you always listen, you are always willing to help, and you make me feel like an equal." Tony thanks him and Rick leaves.

Knock, knock! It is Chad asking Tony if he can speak with him. Tony invites Chad in and asks what he can do for him. Chad says, "I can't help but notice that everyone seems to be coming to you for advice or help with work issues. No one has been to my office for almost two weeks. Do you know why?" Knowing this was coming; Tony swallows hard and says, "I might have some ideas as to what's going on. Do you want me to share them with you?" "Yep, I sure do," replies Chad. Tony tells Chad they will need to go to his office to work this out.

As they enter Chad's office Tony sees a shirt hanging on the coat rack and immediately the rumor about changing shirts in the middle of the day pops into his head. Tony asks, "Can I ask you a question or two?" Chad heartily replies, "Sure, if it will help get to the bottom of what's going on. Fire away!"

Tony asks Chad why he brings a shirt to work and changes halfway through his shift. Chad quickly replies, "So I can look better than my team all day, I'm their boss." As Tony acknowledges Chad, he asks why all his achievement patches are on his shirt. Without hesitation Chad proudly says, "I earned them, and I feel everyone needs to know it." Then Tony asks him what is up with all the awards on his wall and Chad replies, "Again, Tony, I earned all of them and everyone needs to know it, I'm the boss!" Tony walks over to all the photos and asks Chad why there are not any photos of anyone else. Chad snips, "My office, my photos." Chad then tells Tony, "This is my office and everyone that works for me needs to understand why I'm their boss. I want my accomplishments to be the first thing they see when entering my office. It sends a strong message of my Leadership ability and gives them confidence in me."

Tony is silent for a few seconds, clears his throat and says, "Chad, I respectfully disagree. Several of our coworkers complained to me about how intimidating it is to be in your

"Hey, Look at Me" Syndrome

office and how you exude the arrogance of being better than they are." Tony continues by telling Chad that when he walks into his office the first thing that comes to mind is, "Who are you trying to impress, you or me?" Before Chad can respond Tony tells him that he needs to understand that all his coworkers are aware of the measures that must be achieved to be promoted into Leadership. Furthermore, they do not come to him to be reminded; they come to him for *their* benefit. They need guidance and Leadership, not reminding they have not reached the same level of achievement he has.

Tony pulls Chad in front of the full-length mirror next to Chad's desk and says, "If I were you, I would look into this mirror for a while and when you're done, get rid of it. I don't feel you are seeing the true reflection." Red faced Chad stares at Tony and then says, "Yeah, whatever!"

Summary
Do you remember in the last chapter when I said **YOU** are an employee, the same as everyone else? The only difference is your *role.* Yours is Leadership! So, going forward, show up for work every day with the attitude and focus that you are no more or less important than any other employee. You simply have a different role! Do you feel Chad sees himself as an equal employee with the different role of being in Leadership? Of course, he does not. Chad clearly does not view himself as an equal; rather, as being superior to everyone he works with.

Do you feel Tony views himself as an equal employee, with a different role? Of course, he does. Why do you think everyone came to him for assistance and guidance? I will tell you why, they were comfortable (not intimidated) with him and felt they could better relate because Tony sees himself at their level.

Does Tony have the same amount of company award patches, achievement plaques, and certificates that Chad does? Yes, if you recall in the beginning, I told you that each level of leadership in the Woo-Woo company garners a certain level of training. In other words, they all have the same level of expertise and accomplishment to provide the same level of Leadership. The difference is that Tony understands as a leader he is in the Relationship business. Tony does not want to alienate himself from his coworkers by reminding them how great and wonderful he is through constant display of his success. Chad's impersonal display of superiority continues to alienate him from the people he is in charge of leading.

Unless your employer requires you to display patches, pins, ribbons, plaques, and certificates, I encourage you to store them out of sight.

Relationship Leadership **Power Harnessed**
- Trust
- Respect
- Character
- Equality
- Reputation
- Confidence

Take-Away
Be like Tony and *Don't be like Chad!*

Chapter 9

Less Than Perfect

"When nobody around you seems to measure up, it's time to check your yardstick."

-**Bill Lemley**

Janice starts the meeting with Tony and Chad by announcing the annual report will be due soon. She tells them she needs the reports on her desk by noon at the end of the month (31st). Janice proceeds to review the contents of the report, telling them that the 3 components that must be accurate are gross production (number of Woo-Woos produced in the past year), current inventory, and product loss (waste) of each team. There are only two production teams at the Woo-Woo factory with one being assigned to Tony and the other to Chad. After Tony and Chad acknowledge what is expected Janice thanks them for their time and adjourns the meeting.

The next morning Tony meets with Mallory. He tells her the annual report is due in less than a month and because of her stellar work ethic and Leadership he is assigning her the task of preparing the annual report. Tony reviews the three main components that must be accurate and asks her for a rough draft in three weeks. Mallory says she understands and will get right on it! She is excited and honored that Tony is placing so much confidence in her.

At the same time Tony is meeting with Mallory, Chad is meeting with Phil. He tells Phil the annual report is due in less than a month and he is assigning him to prepare the annual report. Chad reviews the three main components with Phil and tells him that Janice said they must be accurate. Then Chad says to Phil, "This is my responsibility to Janice, and I want to be clear that this report must be perfect. I will accept nothing less than flawless! I want a rough draft on my desk in three weeks." Phil acknowledges that he understands and leaves to get started on the task at hand.

Tony answers a knock at his door, and it is Mallory. Three weeks have passed, and she gives Tony a rough draft of the annual report. He asks her to have a seat while he reviews it. Tony knows the crucial information that must be accurate is the three components Janice requires. He previously calculated this information and checks his numbers with the numbers in Mallory's report. She has the correct calculations in her report.

Tony knows nothing is perfect, but he strives to get as close as possible. Tony points to a couple of spelling errors, some sentence structure errors, and a couple of grammar errors and asks Mallory if she will correct them and re-submit the report. She gladly says yes, and the revised report will be on his desk by the end of the day.

Phil knocks at Chad's door and announces he has the annual report done. Chad asks him to come in and have a seat while he reviews the report. Like Tony, Chad knows the correct number for the three main components. He checks these first and tells Phil they are correct. Then Chad says, "Phil, this report is a representation of me, and I thought I was clear that I wanted it perfect – no flaws!" Chad pulls out a red marker and begins marking Phil's report. He is vigorously marking on every page and shaking his head left to right the whole time. Chad finishes and gives the red ink-stained report back to Phil and sternly says, "You need to fix this and get it back to me in two days. The content, sentence structure, spelling, grammar, font, font size, and margins are a train wreck. There is no way I'm turning this into Janice!" Phil tells Chad he will get right on it and have a corrected report to him within two days. Phil walks away so confused that he does not know where to begin the corrections.

The day is near an end, and it is Mallory at Tony's door with a corrected version of the annual report. Tony reviews the corrections he asked Mallory to make, and they are all done. "Good job," says Tony. He thanks Mallory and she returns to work. Tony immediately walks upstairs to Janice's office and turns in his team's annual report…a week early.

Two days have passed, and it is Phil at Chad's door. Chad invites Phil in, and he presents Chad with a corrected report. Chad leans back in his chair and says, "Well Phil, let's see how many of my corrections you got right and how many you screwed up." He takes out his red marker, shakes his head left to right, and commences to marking. Just like last time, Chad marks every page of the report and gives it back to Phil. He tells Phil to have it corrected and back in his office in three days.

Three days later Phil is back in Chad's office with a corrected report. By now you know the drill. Chad starts marking and is not done until he has inked every page. He gives Phil the corrections and says, "Phil, why is it that every time I read this report it seems different than before?" Phil responds by telling Chad he does not know because he is doing everything Chad asks him to. Chad looks at Phil and sternly says. "I need this report cleaned up and on my desk by Monday morning (31st)! I have to turn it in to Janice by noon!" As confused as ever, Phil tells Chad he understands and slowly walks out of the office.

It is 11:30 and Chad is frantic! Phil is not done with the report corrections, and he is meeting with Janice in 30 minutes. Seeing that Phil is not going to get the corrections completed on time, Chad decides to go to the meeting empty handed and assure Janice the report will be done by the end of the day.

It is 12:00 and Janice walks into the conference room where Tony and Chad are waiting. She immediately thanks Tony for having his annual report a week early and tells him it looks good. Janice then takes a deep breath, looks at Chad and says, "I notice you don't have a report for me, do you mind telling me where it is?" Chad tells Janice there are some errors that need correcting to make the report perfect. He continues by telling Janice she will have it by the end of the day. "I better have it by the end of the day, or you are going to have other problems to deal with! Get out of my office and finish your annual report," says Janice.

Tony and Chad are walking down the stairs when Chad asks Tony how he managed to get his report perfected and turned in a week early. "It wasn't perfect," says Tony. Chad then asks why he turned in a report that wasn't perfect and Tony replied, "Chad, nothing is perfect and never will be. Mallory's report is accurate, legible, and easily understood. That is all Janice wanted. *Perfect is an illusion and if you think differently my friend, then you are chasing a rabbit you can't catch."* Chad scoffs, looks at Tony and says, "Yeah, whatever!"

Summary
What do you think Chad accomplished in his pursuit for the perfect annual report? I will tell you; he frustrated Phil, made him feel inadequate, and failed at meeting the deadline. Why do you think Chad said the report seems different each time he reads it? Well, could it be that every time he made corrections, they were so deep that it changed the scope (or feel) of the report? I think so. And what about poor Phil? He was not going to get it right no matter how hard he tried.

What about Tony? Now, he knows perfection is an illusion. Tony recognized some things on Mallory's report he would have done different, but he was not the one doing the report. Mallory was! Tony knew that if he was critical enough, there is always an error that can be found and a correction to be made. He accomplished Janice's request with accurate numbers, a professionally written report, and Mallory feeling good about her accomplishment. Do you think Tony harnessed any *Relationship Leadership* power? Yes!

Let us take a deeper look at the pursuit of perfection. Perfection is an asymptote in the same manner as mastery is an asymptote. An asymptote is basically a curve that approaches a straight line but the two never meet. The same is true of perfection because mastery and perfection is basically the same thing. In his book *Drive,* Daniel Pink writes about the Mastery Asymptote, "Mastery is an asymptote. You can approach it. You can home in on it. You can get really, really close to it. But... you can never touch it. Mastery is impossible to realize fully."[1]

I created a diagram similar to Pink's for you to better understand the visual side of this concept. If you look at the line of *Best Effort* you will see as it approaches *Perfection* the line curves. This represents that as we get better at something we get closer to Perfection. However, this is as close as we are going to get because the two are unable to intersect.[2]

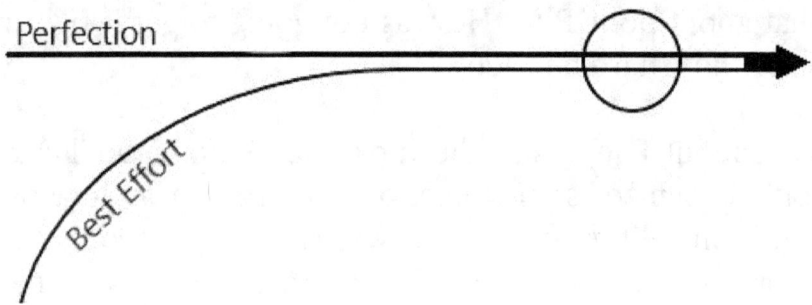

What I want you to do is always focus on the circle. This is where Best Effort travels alongside Perfection. I call this **Less Than Perfect** and it is what you should always strive for in *Relationship Leadership.*

While we are at it, I will do you one better! As much editing this book went through, as many times as I read, re-read, typed and re-typed, I am confident you will find an error or two if you look hard enough. And you know what? I am okay with it! Why? Because as thorough as I am, I understand the sweet spot of *Less Than Perfect*.

Tony gets it and now you do too. Poor Chad is on a merry-go-round in pursuit of perfection. The harder he tries, the faster it goes, and eventually it will throw him. And I do not anticipate a soft landing. As for YOU, please stay off the merry-go-round!

Relationship Leadership **Power Harnessed**
- Trust
- Respect
- Appreciation
- Confidence
- Teamwork
- Empowerment

Take-Away
Be like Tony and *Don't be like Chad!*

CHAPTER 10

Fess Up

"The quality of a leader is reflected in the standards they set for themselves."

-Ray Kroc

Tony and Chad start their day in a meeting with Janice. She called the meeting to explain the new vendor contract and software the Woo-Woo company recently purchased. The new software is used to order from the new vendor, and she plans for the Woo-Woo production line to officially transition to the new supply platform in 60 days.

After explaining the implementation timeline, Janice tells them each team will continue to operate independent of the other. This means responsibility for ordering vendor supplies will remain with the Leadership of each team. Janice tells Tony and Chad they have 30 days to learn the software and then 30 days to order from the vendor. This will ensure all necessary supplies are in stock and ready to go for the 60-day deadline.

Janice looks at Chad and says, "Chad, you've been on thin ice with me lately. I fully expect you to meet my deadline with this transition. This is your chance for redemption, can you get it done?" Chad replies, "Yes ma'am, I am on it and thank you for the chance at redemption." Janice thanks them for their time and adjourns the meeting.

Tony is back in his office and studying the new software manual when Chad knocks on his door. "Come in," says Tony. Chad enters and asks Tony if he has had time to look at the new software manual. "Doing it now, what about you?" asks Tony. Chad says he looked at it and it is a lot to digest. "I think I'm going to assign this to some members of my team and let them figure it out," replies Chad. Tony asks Chad if he thinks that is a good idea and Chad responds with, "Yep, they have to learn about it sooner or later." Tony wishes him luck and Chad leaves.

Tony understands that regardless of success or failure this is his responsibility. If something goes wrong and production must shut down, his team will be at risk of not working until the problem is corrected. He decides that he will learn the software and order from the vendor to meet the 60-day deadline. Going forward, Tony will then design a training program for each team member to complete. Once everyone is proficient, he will transition responsibilities to designated team members.

At their team meeting Tony explains the new software being implemented to order supplies from the new vendor. Additionally, he reviews the 60-day timeline and Janice's expectations. Tony tells his team that he is going to learn the software and order supplies to meet the deadline. "This would be a burden on each of you to learn and meet the 60-day deadline while having to work a full shift," says Tony. He tells them his plan to train everyone and then assign the task to certain team members. It will

Fess Up

then be their responsibility to use the software and maintain the needed amount of inventory for production.

Chad meets with his team and explains the new software being implemented to order supplies from the new vendor. Additionally, he reviews the 60-day timeline and Janice's expectations. Then Chad instructs Phil and Katie to learn the software and order supplies for inventory.

"So, you want us to learn a new software and order from a new vendor all while working our full shift?" asks Katie. Chad responds yes, this is his expectation because they are going to have to learn it anyway. Chad also explains if they do not meet the deadline there will be repercussions. A tad bit pissed, and clearly confused, Chad's team leaves the meeting and goes back to work.

One week before the 60-day deadline Tony is in Janice's office telling her he made an error and his team's transition will be 5 days later than mandated. "Why?" asks Janice. He explains that when he ordered supplies, he did not see the disclaimer in the software of the expected shipping time. With the old system it is 10 days but with the new software and vendor it is 20 days. Tony further explains to Janice that he caught his error a few days ago. Realizing production will shut down from lack of inventory; he ordered enough supplies from the old vendor to bridge the gap of the new vendor supplies arriving. Tony then apologizes for his error.

"I'm disappointed in you Tony. However, I do respect your willingness to admit your error and letting me know before I discovered it on my own. Your forward thinking to cover the supply gap so that we do not shut down production exemplifies your Leadership ability," says Janice. She tells Tony that normally under circumstances like this and because more is expected of Leadership, discipline would be rather severe. Considering his candor and forward thinking, she is going to discipline him with only a written reprimand. Tony gladly accepts the reprimand and thanks Janice for her professionalism.

After leaving Janice's office Tony calls a team meeting. He tells everyone of his error and assures them production will not halt. Tony explains about the disclaimer and how he ordered enough supplies from the old vendor to keep production running. He also wants them to know that he received a written reprimand for not meeting Janice's expectation and he gladly accepted it. "This is my responsibility and I own the error," says Tony. He closes the meeting by thanking his team for their continued hard work and understanding his shortcoming.

Chad arrives for work on day 60. As soon as he walks in the door Katie meets him with a frantic look on her face. "What's wrong?" asks Chad. Katie explains that supplies from the new vendor did not arrive overnight, and the production line will shut down in about an hour due to lack of inventory. "How in the hell did this happen?" screams Chad. Katie further explains that when supplies were ordered, no one saw the new vendor's 20-day shipping time disclaimer. It was not discovered until this morning, when she called the vendor to verify the order.

Chad hustles to Janice's office to let her know what is about to happen. He walks in and tells her his production line will shut down in about an hour. "What?" screams Janice. Chad proceeds to tell her about the error and it will be 10 days before supplies arrive. "Why am I just now being informed about this?" inquires Janice. Chad explains that he delegated the responsibility to Phil and Katie, and he did not know about the error until he arrived at work this morning. "Why did you do that? There is plenty of time to train them and transition responsibility. I specifically gave this task to you, not them," barks Janice.

Chad explains that because this was not his fault, he is going to reprimand Phil and Katie for failing. Janice is seething with anger as she stands, places both hands on her desk, leans toward Chad and says, "Like hell you are and like hell it wasn't your fault! This was your responsibility, not theirs! Because their production line is shut down you just put your team out of work for 10 days! Well, guess what? I am putting you out of work for 10 days! Your suspension starts right now!"

Summary

Do you feel Janice's punishment of Chad was harsh? I do not and I am not sure he does not deserve more than he received. What about Tony? Do you feel his punishment was fair? I do!

Chad never really assumed responsibility for this task. Being in Leadership means he is always responsible for failure and should always own it. Instead, he chose to insulate himself from failure by delegating to Phil and Katie. Chad positioned himself to claim victory if they succeeded and at the same time be able to defer failure from himself by taking disciplinary action against them.

Relationship Leadership

Let us look at how Tony handled the situation. Do you feel he understood that responsibility for failure was his alone? Yeah, me too!

What about being forward thinking enough to order supplies from the old vendor to cover the gap in delivery from the new vendor? Tony took ownership in the wake of failure which prevented production from shutting down and his team being out of work for 5 days.

When Tony told Janice about his error do you think she appreciated him telling her a week in advance? Not only did he own the error, but he also brought her a solution to the problem so she would not have to deal with it.

Do you feel Janice went easier on Tony with discipline because of the way he handled the situation? You bet she did! When you mess up, you *Fess UP!* Tony knew he was going to be disciplined and went to Janice and fell on his sword anyway. This is a crucial Leadership concept I need you to understand. Taking responsibility by getting in front of your mistakes and being totally honest will always serve you better in the discipline arena than playing the blame game and shirking responsibility like Chad. Did Tony harness any *Relationship Leadership* power with Janice? Yes, I am confident that even though Tony messed up, he scored one in the win column with Janice.

What about Tony meeting with his team and telling them he made an error, owning it, and being disciplined? He could have chosen to never tell them what happened. After all, they were not going to be out of work and would be none the wiser of which vendor the supplies came from.

This showed his team that he is just as capable of making mistakes as they are and not any more above being disciplined than they are. Do you think Tony harnessed any *Relationship Leadership* power with his team? Again, yes!

Relationship Leadership Power Harnessed
- Integrity
- Ethics
- Humility
- Respect
- Morals
- Accountability

Take-Away
Be like Tony and *Don't be like Chad!*

Chapter 11

Work Family Warrior

"Nobody cares how much you know, until they know how much you care."

-Theodore Roosevelt

It is the end of the workday as Chad walks by Tony's office and sees he is changing clothes and putting on a suit. He knocks and then walks in to inquire why Tony is putting on the fancy clothes.

"Where are you going all spiffed up?" asks Chad. Tony tells Chad that he is going to Susan and Megan's wedding and reception. Tony then asks Chad if he is going. Chad says, "Nah, I don't do weddings." Tony acknowledges Chad's reluctance to attend and leaves for the wedding.

After a beautiful wedding ceremony Tony is at the reception and walks over to Susan and Megan to congratulate them on their matrimony. Susan asks Tony, "Was Chad at our wedding? I didn't see him." Tony tells Susan he spoke with Chad while leaving work and Chad said he is unable to attend. She says okay, but the disappointment in her voice is unmistakable.

A few days later Chad sees Tony again putting on a suit at the end of the workday. He steps into Tony's office and asks, "Another wedding?" Tony tells him no, that Mike's father passed away and he is going to the funeral. Tony asks Chad if he is going and Chad replies, "Nah, I don't do funerals." Tony acknowledges Chad's reluctance to attend and leaves for the funeral.

After the funeral service and at the burial ceremony, Mike asks Tony if Chad was able to make it. He wants to thank Chad for coming but is unable to find him. Tony tells Mike he spoke with Chad while leaving work and Chad said he is unable to attend. Mike says he understands but was clearly disappointed with Chad's absence.

A couple of weeks later it is Friday afternoon and Chad sees Tony in the hallway. He asks Tony if he has big weekend plans and Tony says yes. "What are you getting into?" asks Chad. Tony tells him that Melanie's daughter is playing in the state championship basketball game, and he has been invited to attend. "Didn't you get an invite?" asks Tony. Chad responds with, "Yeah, but I don't do basketball." Again, Tony acknowledges Chad's reluctance to attend and leaves the conversation.

After the game there is a huge victory celebration. Tony is speaking with Melanie about the game and her daughter's performance when she asks Tony if Chad was able to make it. Tony tells Melanie he spoke with Chad while leaving work and Chad said he is unable to attend. "Oh, okay," Melanie says with somewhat of a said voice.

It is the end of the workday and Chad sees that Tony is carrying a gift wrapped in green paper with golf balls printed on it. He inquires where Tony is going and why is he carrying a gift wrapped in golf ball paper. Tony tells Chad that Courtney is having a birthday party at the local convention center and golf is her favorite sport. "Are you going?" asks Tony. Before he can respond Tony says, "Let me guess. You don't do birthdays." Chad snidely responds, "Yep, you got it!"

The party is first class. A live band, open bar, and a food and dessert buffet. Everyone is dancing and having a good time. Tony and Courtney are on the dance floor when she inquires about Chad's attendance. Tony tells Courtney he spoke with Chad while leaving work and Chad said he is unable to attend. She replies with, "I don't know why I bothered to invite him. He never comes to any personal events and doesn't care about anyone but himself."

Monday morning Chad knocks and walks into Tony's office. "Can I ask you something?" inquires Chad. "Sure," says Tony. "Why do you spend so much of your off time attending coworkers' personal events?" Chad asks. Tony tells Chad that he attends because it is important to show his coworkers that he cares beyond their time together at work. Plus, they make the effort to invite him, which means it is important to them that he attends. "I make the extra effort because it's what Leadership is all about. My genuine concern and sharing in their life events strengthens my relationship with them both personally and professionally. What Leadership message would I be sending if my only focus on coworkers is work and not who they are outside of work?" says Tony. Chad arrogantly responds with, "Time after work is my time and I'm not sharing it with anyone I work with!" Tony silently looks at Chad for a few seconds (while thinking in his mind how Chad does not get that in

Leadership, he is in the Relationship business) and then he says, "No biggie, I understand if it's not about you, you're not interested." Chad is now pissed because he has been called out by Tony. He pauses and decides that he does not have to take such harsh criticism from Tony. Without saying a word, Chad starts swiftly walking away and then suddenly stops at the door; he looks over his shoulder at Tony and sharply says, "Yeah whatever!"

Summary

Do you think Chad harnessed any *Relationship Leadership* power by not making the effort to show his coworkers that he cares about them outside of work? No, me neither!

Can you see how Chad is slowly but surely alienating himself from his coworkers? His self-centered behavior is so toxic that sooner or later no one will be inviting him to any personal events. What is the point, right? He is not going to show up anyway.

How do you think Tony's coworkers feel about his effort to be a part of their personal lives? Do you think they appreciate his genuine concern about the personal side of their lives? Of course, they do!

Do you feel Tony strengthens his working relationship with his coworkers by attending personal events as often as he can? Yeah, me too!

You see, Tony understands that he spends so much work time with his coworkers, they eventually become somewhat of a family. Think about it. Do you feel a special bond with your coworkers? Most of us do because we spend so much time together.

Now, go back to the quote at the beginning of this chapter and let that sink in for a minute or two. Do you really care much about someone if you believe that they do not care about you? No, most of us do not. Do you trust and want to follow someone that does not care? Who does, right?

Many times, I have said that in Leadership you are in the Relationship business. This is a crucial principle that I need to ensure you firmly grasp. Making the effort to be a part of the personal life of those you lead will only strengthen your relationship with them. In turn, this strengthens their desire to accept and follow you as their leader, which strengthens your Leadership effectiveness.

Now, do not go off the rails here and invite yourself to every coworker's personal event. You will look like an idiot trying too hard to be accepted. In time, and as Leadership trust and personal relationships build, you will be invited. I recommend you attend as many as possible. However, remember that you have a personal life to balance as well and occasionally you may have to decline a coworker's personal event. Make sure you inform them of your other commitments and do not leave them wondering why you did not make it.

Remember this; if it is important enough for a coworker to invite you to share in their personal life, it should be important enough for you to make every effort to accept and show your support.

***Relationship Leadership* Power Harnessed**
- Trust
- Acceptance
- Camaraderie
- Respect
- Bonding
- Support

Take-Away
Be like Tony and *Don't be like Chad!*

The Principle of Integrity

Will you follow someone that you can't trust, isn't fair, and doesn't always do the right thing?

CHAPTER 12

The First Dance

"I've learned that people will forget what you said, people will forget what you did, but people will never forget how you made them feel."

-Maya Angelou

It is Friday afternoon and almost quitting time at the Woo-Woo factory. Chad walks into Tony's office and asks him if he is taking a date to the employee appreciation dance tomorrow evening? Every year the company hosts an appreciation dance that includes dinner and an open bar. Tony says, "No, I'm going by myself, I want to be free to dance with everyone. What about you?" Chad says, "Me neither. I asked Rebecca but she's going with a group of friends." "Okay, I'll see you tomorrow evening," says Tony as he closes his office door and heads home.

The dance started at 8:00 p.m. and Chad did not arrive until 9:00. As he walks in, he sees Tony already on the dance floor. However, he is not really interested in watching Tony dance, he wants to find Rebecca and spend time with her. While at the bar (Chad likes to drink) he sees Rebecca and asks her to sit at his table. She agrees and follows him to a seat next to Chad at one of two tables closest to the dance floor. The other table is where Tony sits when he is not dancing.

Chad asks Rebecca to dance, and she agrees. While they are dancing it is obvious that Chad is extremely interested in Rebecca. He is energetic, careful with his steps, leads, and holds her close. Chad is the perfect dance partner to the point that it catches the eye of several single women.

When Rebecca leaves to get a drink, Ashley pounces on the opportunity, and asks Chad for a dance. In his mind he really does not want to, even though Ashley is probably the best-looking woman there. However, he reluctantly says yes. As they dance Chad is not energetic, does not lead, and keeps an arm's length distance (he never gets close). Keep in mind that Chad is handsome and has the interest of several female coworkers, all of whom are watching and waiting to seize their moment to ask Chad for a dance.

After their dance ends, Ashley is clearly disappointed in her dance with Chad. But, before he can get back to his table, Emily approaches him and asks to dance. Again, in his mind Chad really has no interest in Emily and does not really want to dance with her. Reluctantly, he says yes. By now you probably get the picture that Chad only has interest in Rebecca, and it is obvious. Chad dances with Emily the same as he did Ashley. He is kind of like dancing with a giant dead fish, and she is extremely disappointed. Also, the other single women wanting time with Chad noticed how he danced so differently with Ashley and Emily than he did with Rebecca.

The First Dance

Tony, now there is someone that came to dance! He is all over the dance floor, dancing to most every song and with someone different each song. Tony is full of energy, carefully leads, stays close, and is an absolute pleasure to dance with. And guess what? All the women are watching!

As the night wears on Chad is sitting at the table (by himself) and knocking back one drink after the other. While sitting there he begins to watch Tony dance. He notices that Tony's table is full of women sitting and waiting to dance with him. Hell, there is even a small group of women standing and waiting for Tony to return to the table so they can have the next dance.

After a while Chad is feeling the buzz and ready to dance some more. He looks for Rebecca and cannot find her. After a few minutes he sees Ashley standing at Tony's table and walks over and asks her to dance. She says, "No thank you, I'm waiting to dance with Tony." What? He thinks to himself, how can you say no to me and yes to Tony? Chad then walks around the table where Ashley is standing and asks her to dance. She politely says, "No thank you, I'm waiting to dance with Tony." Pissed and dismayed at their refusal, Chad abruptly turns and heads to the restroom.

Upon his return Chad is determined to find Rebecca and dance with her. After all, she is the main reason he came to the dance. Ah-ha! He sees Rebecca sitting at Tony's table. Swiftly and with purpose Chad walks over and asks her to dance. She says, "No thank you, I'm waiting to dance with Tony." Extremely disappointed, pissed, and drunk, Chad calls a cab and leaves.

Monday morning and still a bit pissed, Chad walks into Tony's office and asks if he had a good time at the dance? Tony says, "I had a blast. What about you? I didn't see you dance much." Chad sharply responds, "No kidding! It seemed as if every woman wanted to dance with you! I even saw you dance with a few women that I didn't think you were very fond of." "What do you mean?" questions Tony. Chad tells him he is confused. "You danced every time with the same enthusiasm and vigor. Have you forgotten that you recently disciplined Shelly for tardiness, gave Brittany a poor performance review, and Tiffany is on probation for her attitude?" asks Chad. Tony says, "Yeah, I knew all this before we danced. However, all that is in the past, and I treat everyone with the same respect. They asked me to share time with them by dancing and their past work performance had nothing to do with me giving each one an equal amount of my time and energy on the dance floor." Chad kind of snarled and abruptly walks away as he says, "Yeah, whatever."

Summary

Have you ever had someone in a Leadership position treat you differently than other coworkers? Especially after a negative encounter with them? Most of us have.

You see, Tony may not have been pleased with his coworkers' performance, tardiness, and attitude issues, but that is not the point here. I am sure they were not too happy about being part of their corrective actions either. However, Tony chose to neutralize his feelings and treat everyone the same.

How do you think Tony made Shelly, Brittany, and Tiffany feel when he danced with them? Despite their previous discipline issues, Tony gave each of them the same amount of dance that he gave everyone else. Do you think Shelly, Brittany, and Tiffany felt better about working with Tony after being treated equal to the coworkers that did not have previous discipline issues? Also, what do you think the chances are they will reciprocate positive behavior toward Tony going forward?

What about Chad? He was clearly focused on Rebecca and no one else. Do you think Chad deals with his coworkers the same way he dealt with them at the dance? I am betting the answer is yes. While talking with Tony, his bias toward the other coworkers that recently had negative issues at work was obvious. Do you think they will reciprocate negative behavior toward Chad?

Being able to sterilize his emotions and treat everyone the same, whether at work or play, Tony develops a positive Relationship with every coworker. Chad's indifference hinders him from building strong Relationships with his coworkers because he does not understand the equality he must foster and maintain to be an effective leader.

Relationship Leadership **Power Harnessed**
- Equality
- Respect
- Acceptance
- Integrity
- Impartial
- Consideration

Take-Away
Be like Tony and *Don't be like Chad!*

Chapter 13

Giving Credit

"A good leader is a person who takes a little more than his share of the blame and a little less than his share of the credit."

-John Maxwell

Chad is quietly eating lunch (by himself) at the table behind Jackie and Sandy. Unknown to them, he can hear every word and is conveniently eavesdropping!

Jackie is telling Sandy that she figured out a way to get two more Woo-Woos in each box during final packaging. She continues telling Sandy exactly how the configuration needs to be and how her idea should reduce packaging cost. Chad is all ears and as Jackie is explaining to Sandy, he is working through her idea on a napkin. It didn't take long for him to realize she was right; it will work!

Sandy tells Jackie that she needs to share her idea with Chad, since he is their team leader. Jackie is naturally shy and rarely speaks up about work issues. She is reluctant to tell Chad and instead tells Sandy she should share the idea with Chad. Sandy refuses and tells Jackie it's her idea and

Relationship Leadership

she should get credit. Jackie agrees and tells Sandy she'll share with Chad when they are done eating lunch.

Jackie is in Chad's office waiting for him to return from lunch when he walks in and asks her why she's in his office. She tells him that she wants to bounce an idea off him. Jackie continues telling Chad that she discovered a way to reduce packing costs. "If we arrange the finished product into a different configuration, we can get two more Woo-Woos in each box," says Jackie. She is explaining the new configuration when Chad interrupts her and says, "I'm not sure this will work but I will run it by Janice and let's see what she says. I'll get back with you as soon as I can." He then asks her if there is anything else she needs to discuss because he has work to do. Jackie says no and as she gets up to leave Chad thanks her for sharing and again expresses his doubt. She walks out of Chad's office feeling the sting of self-doubt.

As soon as Jackie leaves Chad immediately begins working on a written proposal to present to Janice (CEO). Chad knows Jackie's idea will work and it's his opportunity to score one in the win column with Janice. He is going to make sure this idea gets endorsed by upper management and he is recognized for bringing it forward.

Janice walks into the conference room and inquires why Chad requested to meet with her. He tells Janice that he is confident there is a better way to package Woo-Woos. Chad continues by telling her this idea will increase product quantity in each box by two and in turn reduce packaging cost. Chad tells Janice that he is so confident of this idea that he formalized it in a proposal complete with step-by-step instructions and diagrams. She carefully reviews the proposal and tells Chad she likes the idea. Janice informs him that she is going to send his proposal to engineering for additional testing. If their tests show this idea to be accurate, training and implementation will be scheduled with the Leadership staff as soon as possible.

Before Janice adjourns their meeting, she pauses, looks at Chad and says, "Chad, I'm impressed with this idea and your proposal. This is what I'm looking for in our Leadership staff. You may have just knocked this one out of the park. I am proud of your forward thinking and finding new ways for our company to be more profitable." Chad thinks to himself, "finally!" He thanks Janice for her kind words and returns to his office so he can gloat over his newfound favor with Janice.

Knock, knock! Tony responds and invites Shelly into his office. "What's up?" says Tony. Shelly asks if she can have a few minutes of his time to discuss an idea. Tony stops what he's doing, gives her his undivided attention and tells Shelly he's ready when she is. Shelly explains that she discovered a way to increase efficiency on the production line. Excited and with great interest, Tony asks Shelly to explain her discovery.

Now Tony knows that although Shelly is not employed as an engineer, she has a background in supply chain engineering. Shelly is one of their best and brightest and when she wants to share her expertise, he listens!

Shelly explains that by reformatting the auto assembly software, Woo-Woos can be placed six inches closer during assembly. This will increase production of units per hour and increase efficiency without adding expense to the production process. She further explains that she has been working on the software coding and believes she has it finalized. The final step is to recode the software and do a test run, for which she needs his permission. Tony immediately gives his permission and tells Shelly to report back to him when her testing is complete. Riddled with excitement, she thanks Tony and tells him she will start recoding and testing immediately.

Two days later Shelly is in Tony's office to share the great news. She tells Tony that she tested the software recoding and the closer placement of Woo-Woos during assembly and it worked flawlessly. Tony tells Shelly how much he appreciates her bringing forward such a great idea and wanting to work through testing to completion. He informs Shelly that he will schedule a meeting with Janice (CEO) for her to explain the idea and test results. Shelly is elated with Tony for his support and including her in the meeting with Janice.

Two weeks later Tony and Shelly are in a meeting with Janice. Tony tells Janice that Shelly came up with an awesome idea to increase production line assembly and efficiency. Also, that she conducted extensive testing, and everything works as Shelly envisioned. Janice then asks Shelly to thoroughly explain her idea and testing. As Shelly is explaining her idea and testing Janice is asking questions. Shelly is on point with a quick and thorough answer to every question. After several minutes Janice expresses her satisfaction and tells Tony and Shelly that she will send everything to engineering for additional testing. If their

Giving Credit

tests show Shelly's tests to be accurate, training and implementation will be scheduled with the Leadership staff as soon as possible. Janice thanks both for their time and initiative.

A month later Janice meets with Tony and Chad to inform them of training and implementation dates for the new packaging and assembly processes. It's a brief meeting because, assuming they both know, she doesn't discuss how the ideas came to fruition.

While walking downstairs to their offices Tony congratulates Chad on bringing the packaging idea to Janice. In turn, Chad congratulates Tony on bringing the assembly idea to Janice. Without hesitation Tony says, "Oh, it wasn't my idea, it was Shelly's."

Tony meets with his team to inform them of the training and implementation dates for the two new processes. Everyone is aware the assembly idea is Shelly's, and each team member congratulates her.

Chad meets with his team to inform them of the training and implementation dates for the two new processes. Everyone is aware the packaging idea is Jackie's, and each team member congratulates her. Chad makes no effort to tell his team that Janice doesn't know its Jackie's idea.

Several months into implementation both ideas are working great. Considering this, the annual company dinner is Saturday and Jackie, and Shelly are hoping to receive the annual employee innovation award given to the

111

employee that brings forward the best improvement idea of the year.

The bar is open; everyone has eaten and is mingling. The buzz amongst the employees is who will win the award. From the conversations being had it seems to be about a 50/50 split between Jackie and Shelly. Janice brings attention and asks everyone to be seated for employee recognition awards. Janice tells everyone how much she appreciates their hard work and dedication for a year well done. As she works toward the announcement, she tells the crowd that two ideas were so strong this year, she decided there will be co-innovation award winners.

Janice announces, "Shelly, please come forward and receive the innovation award for the assembly idea." Everyone cheers and Shelly excitedly accepts the award. She takes a minute at the podium to thank her coworkers and Tony for supporting her idea.

Jackie is squirming with anticipation when Janice announces, "Chad, please come forward and receive the innovation award for the packaging idea." Jaws drop as the production staff stares at each other in disbelief. You could have heard a pin drop! Chad walks to the podium and accepts the award. As soon as he makes a brief statement thanking everyone for supporting the idea, several low roaring boo's fill the room. At the same time, emotionally distraught and crying, Jackie gets up and leaves. Janice leans over to Tony and quietly asks, "What the hell was that all about?" Tony says, "I have no clue, but I'm pretty confident Chad does."

Giving Credit

Well, Janice is familiar enough with Chad to know asking him first is not the best way to get to the bottom of issues that involve him. She spends the rest of the evening working the room, inquiring why Chad was booed and Jackie abruptly left crying. It didn't take long for her to understand the packaging idea came from Jackie. While Janice is working the room, Chad realizes he is being ratted out. He quietly slips out the side door and heads home. After several conversations Janice is so upset with Chad that she can't see straight. She looks to confront him but can't find him. Rest assured Monday is not going to be a good day for Chad.

It's Monday morning and Chad is sitting in Janice's office. She walks in, slams her hand on the desk, points her finger at Chad and yells, "You have about two minutes to tell me the truth about the packaging idea and if you tell me the slightest lie, I am firing your ass!" Chad takes a deep breath and explains the idea was Jackie's. "Then why in the hell did you tell me it was your idea?" asks Janice. Chad sharply replies, "I didn't, I never said it was my idea. I just didn't tell you it was Jackie's either." Janice says, "You're damn right you didn't, but the way you presented it implied it was your idea." Chad softly apologizes for what he claims was a misunderstanding. Janice on the other hand, is not quite seeing this as a misunderstanding. She orders Chad to leave her office, go straight to his office and return immediately with the innovation award. "I'm stripping you of this award and giving it to the person that actually earned it," says Janice.

Tuesday afternoon Janice held a companywide meeting and apologized for the misunderstanding as she presented

Jackie with the Innovation Award. Everyone cheered and Jackie finally got the recognition she deserved. Chad didn't attend the meeting; he left work early that day.

Summary
Do you think Chad should be fired for pulling this stunt? Yeah, me too! However, I need him to remain in a Leadership position for the rest of this book so you can learn how *Relationship Leadership* principles work and how to benefit from using them. The more he screws up, the more opportunity for you to learn!

It is clear here what Chad did, but let's dig a bit deeper. He thought he could gain favor with Janice by serving up Jackie's idea without saying it was her idea. If you go back and read the interaction between Janice and Chad, he never actually says it is his idea either. He presented things in a manner that created a logical presumption it was his. This was very deceptive, but in his mind, he wasn't taking any recognition away from Jackie, nor was he giving any. He seized an opportunity to find favor with Janice and deprived Jackie of the recognition she was due for her innovation.

Do you feel Chad harnessed any *Relationship Leadership* power with his team over this shenanigan? No, of course not. What Chad doesn't understand is that employees talk (we discussed this earlier in the book) and not only does his team hate him for this stunt, the whole company does.

What about Tony? From the beginning he included Shelly in the process of taking her idea to the CEO. Not once did he try to divert any credit his direction. It was total recognition for Shelly, and this is how it should always be.

Do you feel Tony harnessed any *Relationship Leadership* power with his team? You bet! Everyone in the company knew Shelly discovered the assembly idea and everyone knew Tony gave her 100% of the credit. Yes, everyone. Why? Because, again, they talk!

What I need you to understand here is to give credit where credit is due 100% of the time. Even if you feel you deserve a little recognition, pass as much credit as possible to everyone involved. The bigger picture here is that if everyone under your Leadership gets credit and you get none, you still benefit from the *Relationship Leadership* power you will harness.

Let's take a different view before we head into the next chapter. Jackie is not in Janice's *Impact Circle*. The only way she can get an idea across the finish line is through Chad. He is the vehicle to do so because he is in Janice's *Impact Circle*. In this scenario Chad saw an opportunity to grab the checkered flag and do a victory lap. Unfortunately, he crashed. NEVER grab someone else's checkered flag because sooner or later you will have one hell of a crash during your victory lap!

Relationship Leadership Power Harnessed
- Trust
- Ethics
- Recognition
- Integrity
- Respect
- Appreciation

Take-Away
Be like Tony and *Don't be like Chad!*

Chapter 14

Credibility

"Integrity is doing what is right and truthful, and doing as you say you would do."

-Roy T. Bennett

Chelease sees Chad walking toward her and stops to invite him out for drinks after work. It's been a hard week and the team is meeting at the local bar to socialize and unwind. Chad says, "Yeah sounds great, I'll see you there."

The team has been at the bar for about an hour when Ayame asks if anyone invited Chad. "I thought he was meeting us," she says. Chelease tells everyone she invited Chad and he said he would be here. The night wears on and everyone has an awesome time. They call it quits at midnight with Chad never showing up.

It's Monday morning and Yolanda knocks on Chad's door and tells him they will be out of ink in about 2 hours. She asks if he can get them a fresh supply and he says, "Sure, I'll get it shortly." The ink is needed to print labels for packaging and is kept in the supply room. Only supervisors have access.

About an hour and half later Yolanda knocks on Tony's door and asks if he can get her some ink for packaging. She tells Tony that she asked Chad, but he has yet to get it and they'll be out real soon. Tony says, "Sure, I'll get right on it." He stops what he's doing and gets the ink.

Chad never got the ink for Yolanda and never said anything to her about it. This was a crucial request to prevent the production line from shutting down. After making the commitment to Yolanda, Chad was a no show!

A few weeks later, employee tardiness is on the rise and to curtail the problem Janice is instituting a companywide progressive discipline policy. She meets with Tony and Chad and tasks them with briefing each member of their team. She is very adamant that the policy be enforced.

The next day Tony and Chad have a joint meeting with their teams to discuss the new policy. Tony explains that anyone tardy two or more times within 30 days will be in violation. This is a progressive discipline policy and additional violations will be met with additional discipline, all the way to termination. Chad chimes in with his support of the new policy and admonishes his team as well. There is some discussion and a few questions, of which Tony and Chad answer. Everyone understands the expectation and consequences.

After 30 days Robert and Jessica were late two times each. They are on Tony's team, and he issues both a written warning for violating the new tardiness policy.

Credibility

On Chad's team Beverly and Elizabeth were late two times each. Chad never mentions it to either of them and takes no action to enforce the new tardiness policy.

Well, as you know by now, word travels! Robert and Jessica are in Tony's office raising hell about being disciplined and want to know why Beverly and Elizabeth were not. Tony tells Robert and Jessica they were disciplined for violating the policy. "I explained the policy and consequences to everyone. It's my job to enforce the policy equally. I told everyone what will happen for violations, and I did exactly as I said I would," replies Tony. He continues explaining that he is not in charge of Chad's team and can't make him enforce policy. It's an administrative matter between Chad and Janice.

Tony realizes the new tardiness policy coupled with the lack of equal discipline (Chad's failure) created a bit of tension. He has an idea to shift the focus toward something positive and hopes Chad follows his lead.

At their weekly team meeting Tony tells everyone that if they exceed last month's production by ten percent, he will buy everyone lunch. Veda asks if it can be a pizza party and Tony agrees. Pizza party it is!

Chad hears about Tony's offer to buy lunch and calls a team meeting. During the meeting Chad tells everyone that Tony is throwing a pizza party if his team meets a ten percent production increase for the month. Chad makes the same offer, and everyone is excited.

A month later Veda knocks on Tony's door and says she checked the production numbers for last month and their team is up ten percent. "Awesome, sounds like I owe you guys a pizza party," replies Tony. He asks her to schedule it for Friday at noon and puts her in charge of coordinating the party.

Terry knocks on Chad's door and says he checked the production numbers for last month and their team is up ten percent. "That's good," replies Chad. Terry reminds him of the promise for a pizza party and says that Veda is coordinating Tony's party for Friday. He volunteers to do the same for their team and Chad says, "No, let's wait for now and I'll get back with you."

It's Friday, the end of the work week and pizza party time! Veda decorated the cafeteria, and the pizza arrives right on time. Tony briefly addresses his team by congratulating them on reaching the goal and thanks them for their commitment to working and winning as a team. He grabs the first slice, takes a big bite, and sits down to celebrate.

On the other side of the cafeteria Chad's team is watching Tony's team celebrate. Terry informs the team that he offered to coordinate their pizza party and Chad said he will get back with him. Chelease asks Terry if Chad said anything else since and he says no, not a word! Chelease rants, "Chad is a horrible boss. He never keeps his word and never follows thru on anything." Ayame chimes in and says, "Tony always does what he says, when he says, and how he says. He is the most credible person I know." Terry takes his turn and says, "Tony is Mr. *Credibility* and Chad is Mr. No *Credibility*!"

Credibility

As you probably guessed by now, Chad never got back with Terry and the pizza party never happened.

Summary

I could write several more pages of scenarios about how Tony gets it right and Chad doesn't. But I'm pretty sure you get the picture by now.

Let's look at Chad's behavior. Do you think he harnessed any power by pulling a no show for after work drinks? Absolutely not! This was an awesome opportunity to bond with his coworkers. Instead, Chad sent the message that he was not a man of his word, and they weren't important enough for him to attend.

What about having total control over the ink, telling your coworker you'll take care of it, and then not do it? They were at his mercy to ensure the ability to keep working and he failed them. How do you think this made them feel about relying upon him in the future?

What about being tardy? Do you feel by not disciplining Beverly and Elizabeth when he said he would that Chad cast himself in the light of poor Leadership? Again, yes! He didn't follow through and guess what? They talk! All employees at the Woo-Woo factory knew it.

How about the pizza party? How would you like to be promised a pizza party for achieving a goal, achieve the goal, and then no party? To make it worse, how would you feel about Chad if you had to sit across the cafeteria and watch your coworkers enjoy their pizza party knowing you met the same goal and were promised the same pizza party? That would suck, wouldn't it?

Now let's look at how Tony handled things. When Yolanda asked Tony to get her some ink, he knew she didn't have access to it. Tony stopped what he was doing and immediately handled her request. By being so responsive do you think Yolanda felt she can depend on Tony in the future? Yep, you better believe it!

Although disciplining someone is never pleasant for either party, it's a part of Leadership. Tony told everyone on his team his expectations and consequences. When Robert and Jackie violated the policy, Tony kept his word and did exactly as he said he would. Do you feel he harnessed any *Relationship Leadership* power by being the disciplinarian? Yes, he did! Although unpleasant, Tony was seen as a man of his word and strong enough to carry through with his commitment. I'm pretty sure he didn't like it but to be credible as a leader it had to be done. Understand that not everyone has the fortitude to carry through with unpleasant actions. However, if you are seen as someone that has this ability, you will be revered and respected.

What about the pizza party? As soon as Veda told Tony they met their production goal his immediate response was, "Awesome, sounds like I owe you guys a pizza party," She didn't have to remind him. Why? Because Tony knew he made a commitment, and it was his responsibility to follow through. Do you feel he harnessed any *Relationship Leadership* power? Yes!

What I need you to understand is that *Credibility* always equals *Honesty and Action.* To build (yes, I said build) *Credibility* you must always be honest and always take the action you commit to. Anything less and you run the risk of a permanent seat on the *Credibility* struggle bus.

Relationship Leadership **Power Harnessed**
- Trust
- Respect
- Honesty
- Dependability
- Reverence
- Attentiveness

Take-Away
Be like Tony and *Don't be like Chad!*

Chapter 15

Why You're the Leader

*"Anyone can hold the helm
when the sea is calm."*

- Publilius Syrus

Demetrius is having trouble with the belt alignment of the Woo Maker 5000. This is causing production to occasionally shut down and is frustrating everyone. After attempting re-alignment several times, he decides it is time for help. Demetrius knows Chad is a certified Woo Maker 5000 machine adjuster. He stops the futile effort and heads to Chad's office.

Knock knock! Chad barks, "Come in." Demetrius enters and asks Chad if he has time to help him with the alignment issue. "What's the problem?" Chad abruptly asks. Demetrius explains the issue as best he can. He's not a certified Woo Maker 5000 machine adjuster like Chad and doesn't completely understand all the adjustment nuances (In other words, he's learning).

Chad snips at Demetrius by telling him that if he's operating the machine, he should know how to repair it. Then he says, "I don't have time to stop what I'm doing every time you have a problem on the production line. If you don't know what you're doing, maybe someone else should be operating the machine." Demetrius apologizes and tells Chad he will improve.

With a frustrated demeanor Chad tells Demetrius to have a seat. He explains in detail how to diagnose and repair the alignment issue. However, Chad's explanation is at the certified adjuster level and way above what Demetrius knows (remember, he is still learning). Chad goes so far as to explain repair issues that Demetrius didn't need to know to repair the machine. This only confuses Demetrius more. Dazed and confused he thanks Chad for his time and leaves.

Knock knock! Tony says, "Come in." Demetrius walks in and asks him if he has a minute to help him with an issue. Tony stops what he's doing and says, "Sure, what's up?" Demetrius tells him about the alignment issue and that he went to Chad for help but now he's more confused than when the problem started. "He talked to me as if I was a 20-year veteran and knew everything about the Woo Maker 5000. If I knew I wouldn't ask. I simply need help," explains Demetrius. Tony asks Demetrius if he can show him what the issue is.

While standing at the Woo Maker 5000 Tony asks Demetrius to show him what he believes the problem is and what he's done to repair it. Demetrius explains his diagnosis and what he did to correct the problem. Tony then says, "No biggie. Here's your problem, these two screws are out of adjustment." Demetrius explains that he turned both screws a quarter turn to the right, but it didn't resolve the issue. "Did you turn them at the same time?" asks Tony. Demetrius says he did not. Tony grabs two

Why You're the Leader

screwdrivers and turns both screws a quarter turn to the right at the same time. "Now, start her up," says Tony. Demetrius hit the power button and the Woo Maker 5000 runs flawlessly. "Wow! I didn't know you can turn both at the same time!" says Demetrius. Tony pats Demetrius on the shoulder and says, "It's just a little trick of the trade I learned from my time on the production floor. Let me know if you need help with anything else." Demetrius thanks Tony for his time and attention to the matter and returns to work.

A couple of days later Demetrius notices that Blake seems to be frustrated about something. He walks toward Blake to investigate. When Demetrius asks Blake what's going on, Blake explains that the taping machine keeps jamming and the packaging is all screwed up. Blake says, "Screw it! I don't know how to fix it so I'm going to Chad for help." Demetrius immediately says, "Hold on a minute, I think you need to go see Tony." "Why?" asks Blake. Demetrius explains his recent encounter with Chad for help and how Chad's attitude was that he should know how to make repairs. Further, Chad's explanation was so over his head that he was more confused than when he asked for help. Demetrius went on to explain how Tony stopped what he was doing and came to the production floor to see for himself. And, as a result, Demetrius learned a "trick of the trade." Blake agreed and went to see Tony.

Again, Tony stopped what he was doing and went to see for himself. After a few minutes working with the taping machine Tony had it running flawlessly. While helping Blake with the repair Tony also took time to explain and show him how to resolve the problem. "Wow! Thanks boss!

Now I can fix it next time," says Blake. Tony tells him he's welcome, and everyone went back to work.

About a week later Blake and Demetrius see that Danielle is having trouble with the separator on the Woo Maker 5000. They walk over and ask her about it, and she says, "Yeah, I'm not sure what the problem is or how to fix it." Danielle then tells them that the buzz around the lunch table is to not ask Chad for help because he is no help. However, she heard Tony is on vacation. Blake quickly chimes in and says, "No he's not. Tony returned to work today." Relieved, Danielle heads for Tony's office.

As he did with Demetrius and Blake, Tony stopped what he was doing and went to the production floor to help Danielle. After a few minutes he had everything up and running. Danielle is very grateful that Tony helped, and that she also learned how to resolve the issue.

Later that afternoon there's a knock at Tony's door. It's Chad. Tony tells him to come in and asks, "What's up?" Chad seems a bit pissed as he asks Tony why everyone seems to be coming to him for help with production floor repair issues. Before he can answer Chad rants, "I don't understand. If they work in production, they should know how to repair things. If I know it, they should too!" After Chad finishes his rant Tony tells him just because someone works here doesn't mean they know everything. Chad then barks, "Well, I'm a certified Woo Maker 5000 machine adjuster and I know!" Being a little frustrated with Chad's arrogance, Tony says, "You're exactly right! You know but they don't! Your coworkers are coming to you for help, and you barely give them the time of day. Because YOU do know is part of the reason you are in Leadership!" Chad stares at Tony for a few seconds and then walks away. As he gets to the door Chad mumbles, "Yeah, whatever."

Summary
Well, here we go again! As I said earlier, Chad's arrogance is so strong that he can't get out of his own way. Just because he knows, he feels everyone else should. As someone in Leadership do you feel this way? If so, then you're in for the same ride of discontent from your coworkers that Chad is on.

Do you feel Chad harnessed any *Relationship Leadership* power with his arrogance, explaining above the understanding of his coworker and not willing to get out from behind his desk to physically assess the problem? Of course not! As a leader do you feel it is Chad's responsibility to share and teach what he knows? Yes, it is!

What about Tony? Do you feel he harnessed any *Relationship Leadership* power by stopping what he was doing and physically assessing the problem? Of course, he did. Do you feel Tony harnessed any *Relationship Leadership* power by taking the time to teach his coworkers how to resolve the problem? Again, yes!

You see, Tony knows his responsibility as a leader is to always take time to teach someone when they don't know. If he does this everyone benefits. Do you think in the future a coworker will ask for help if they already know how to resolve the problem? Of course not. And, your coworkers will help each other resolve the issue before bringing it to you. In turn, you benefit as a leader because your coworkers are functioning, growing, and learning together.....as a team!

Understand that it is your responsibility as a leader to never assume someone knows just because you do. Anytime you can help or teach someone, seize the opportunity! Remember you are the leader for a reason. If they ask, it is simply because they need YOUR help!

***Relationship Leadership* Power Harnessed**
- Trust
- Respect
- Cooperation
- Attentiveness
- Teamwork
- Teaching

Take-Away
Be like Tony and *Don't be like Chad!*

Chapter 16

The Second Dance

"The supreme quality of leadership is integrity."

- Dwight Eisenhower

Bethany is the floor supervisor and notices that Rebecca didn't show up for work. Concerned, she calls her to see if something is wrong and gets no answer. Bethany asks everyone on the team if they heard from Rebecca and no one has. Since Chad is their leader, she decides to let Chad know of the unapproved absence.

Knock, knock! "Come in," says Chad. Bethany walks in and tells Chad about Rebecca's absence. "I called and got no answer. Then I asked and no one on the team has heard from her," Bethany explains. Chad tells her he will investigate Rebecca's absence and take care of it. Chad knows that any unapproved absence is an automatic one day suspension without pay. However, if you remember in Chapter 12, we learned that Chad really likes Rebecca.

The next day Chad calls Rebecca into his office to investigate her absence. When asked why she was absent Rebecca leans across the desk toward Chad and flirtingly replies, "No real reason. I just wanted the day off and didn't want to go through the hassle of asking for it." Chad replies by telling Rebecca how she violated company policy and can be punished with a one-day suspension. However, Chad flirtingly says, "I think we can overlook your absence just this one time." Rebecca leans a little further across Chad's desk, giggles, and says, "Thanks boss." Chad giggles and replies, "You are welcome....Rebecca." The two maintain eye contact while Rebecca backs out of Chad's office and blows him a kiss just before she exits. Chad blows her a kiss in return, but she's already gone.

Later that afternoon everyone is talking at the lunch table about Rebecca's absence. Katie asks if anyone knows why Rebecca didn't get the mandatory one-day suspension and a few people have an opinion. "Chad likes her more than he does us," snaps Dayshia. "Yeah, he always plays favorites," says Courtney. Susan chimes in with, "Maybe we should flirt with him and then we can do what we want without getting into trouble." Elizabeth stands up and says, "You know what? If she can, so can I! I'm taking Monday off and not telling anyone, nor asking for approval." Nick immediately pipes up and says to Elizabeth, "Pump your brakes princess. You do realize we are on Tony's team, don't you?" She says it shouldn't matter whose team she is on because if one employee can do it they all should be able to. "Well, good luck with that," replies Nick.

Monday morning rolls around and guess who is not at work? Elizabeth! Megan is the floor supervisor and notices Elizabeth didn't show up for work. Concerned, she calls her to see if something is wrong and gets no answer. Megan asks everyone on the team if they heard from

The Second Dance

Elizabeth and no one has. Since Tony is their leader she decides to let Tony know of the unapproved absence.

Knock, knock! "Come in," says Tony. Megan walks in and tells Tony about Elizabeth's absence. "I called and got no answer. Then I asked and no one on the team has heard from her," Megan explains. Tony tells her he will handle it and thanks her for bringing it to his attention.

Tuesday morning Tony tells Megan to send Elizabeth to his office as soon as she arrives. Shortly after, Tony hears a knock at the door and responds with, "Come in." As she enters Elizabeth says, "Hey boss, do you need to see me about something?" Tony asks her to have a seat and inquires about her unapproved absence the day before. Elizabeth very confidently states, "Well, we all know Rebecca didn't get in trouble for her unapproved absence. I wanted yesterday off so I took it....just like she did." Tony firmly explains to Elizabeth, "Chad is not the leader of our team, I am. And, you are not on Chad's team, you are on ours." Tony continues by telling her that he can't control how Chad leads. "When it comes to leading our team, I have a responsibility to be fair and equitable to everyone....and I will," says Tony. As Elizabeth begins to tear up Tony tells her that per company policy, and effective immediately, she will receive a one-day suspension without pay. He ends the meeting and sends Elizabeth home to begin her suspension.

What you need to know here is that Elizabeth is an excellent employee. Although their relationship is strictly platonic, Tony considers them close friends.

It's Wednesday and lunch time. Katie, Dayshia, Courtney, Susan and Nick are sitting at the table when Elizabeth walks up and has a seat. "Well, I saw you weren't here Monday. How did that work out for you?" asks Nick. Elizabeth snaps at Nick with, "Not very well! I got a one-day suspension without pay! I don't understand, Rebecca and Chad are friends, and nothing happened to her. Tony and I are friends and I got suspended!" Nick responds with, "Oh this is really simple! Tony is our leader and Chad is not much of a leader. Friends or not, Tony had a job to do with your discipline and he did it. It's what leaders do!"

Later that day Chad is walking down the hall toward the restroom when he hears someone talking (really loud). He stops to listen without making his presence known. It's Priscilla and she seems to be gossiping about a coworker. Chad listens long enough to confirm his suspicion and then interrupts the conversation. He immediately tells Priscilla to follow him to his office.

There are two things you need to know here. First, Chad dislikes Priscilla. He has wanted to terminate her for a long time. Second, Janice (CEO) recently issued a companywide policy against gossiping and expects it to be rigidly enforced. The first violation carries discipline of two days suspension without pay and a written letter of apology to the offended party.

Chad explains to Priscilla that he overheard her gossiping about a coworker and is going to discipline her for violating company policy. He tells Priscilla that he is terminating her pending Janice's approval. Sniffling and wiping the tears out of her eyes Priscilla says, "You can't do that! Termination is

The Second Dance

not the discipline for gossiping." Chad replies, "Well, for you Priscilla, I think it should be!" He instructs her to wait in his office and heads upstairs to get approval from Janice.

After waiting for Janice to finish a phone call, Chad is invited in. "What's up?" asks Janice. Chad explains that he overheard Priscilla gossiping and wants to terminate her. He cheerfully says, "She is waiting in my office and as soon as you approve, I will gladly deliver her fate." Janice quickly fires back with, "What in the hell do you mean terminate her? The discipline for this violation is not termination." Chad responds by telling Janice that Priscilla is not a good employee, and he dislikes her. He thinks the company needs to cut their losses now. Janice stares at Chad with disbelief for a couple of seconds and then sternly says, "Good employee or not and whether you like her or not has nothing to do with it. We have a policy, she violated the policy, and she will be disciplined per the policy. No more or less than any other employee. We don't selectively enforce policy violations to serve our personal bias." Janice tells Chad to return to his office and discipline Priscilla per the policy and nothing more.

Chad walks into his office, looks at Priscilla and says, "Well, I guess it's your lucky day. Janice said that I can't terminate you for gossiping." He suspends Priscilla immediately and instructs her that she must return to work after two days with a letter of apology.

Just a few days after Priscilla returns to work it seems that the gossip policy has reared its ugly head again. Jasmine (supervisor) sees Randal and Charlie in an argument on the production floor and investigates. She learns that Charlie

Relationship Leadership

heard Randal was gossiping about him during lunch hour and confronted him. Jasmine asks Randal if it is true, and he reluctantly confirms her inquiry. Jasmine tells Randal to follow her to Tony's office.

Knock, knock! Tony answers and Jasmine and Randal enter. As Randal stands with his head hung in shame Jasmine tells Tony that Randal was gossiping about Charlie. Tony asks Randal, "Is this true?" Randal sighs and says, "Yes sir." After a brief discussion of Randal's behavior and policy violation, Tony informs Randal that he is suspended for two days.....effective immediately. Additionally, Tony instructs Randal to bring a letter of apology when he returns to work. Randal apologizes for his misconduct and heads home for the day.

What you need to know here is that Tony is not a big fan of Randal due to disagreements they had in the past. Personally, Tony feels Randal should be given the opportunity to be successful somewhere other than the Woo-Woo factory. He also knows that Randal's termination is not his decision to make.

Summary
Oh, that Chad! Do you feel he harnessed any *Relationship Leadership* power by not disciplining Rebecca? No, of course not. Do you feel he pissed off everyone on his team by giving Rebecca a free pass? I think so! It's no secret he really likes her.

What about Priscilla? Do you feel Chad handled her situation with fairness? No, of course not. When word gets out (and it will because *they talk*) how do you think everyone is going to feel about Chad's Leadership (or lack of)? I'm guessing they are going to be even more pissed when everyone finds out he tried to go above the policy and terminate Priscilla. Chad's dislike for her is no secret.

Now let's look at how Tony handled things. Do you feel he harnessed any *Relationship Leadership* power by not letting his friendship get in the way and disciplining Elizabeth? Yes, he did. Everyone knows they are close friends, but Tony stayed the course by treating her no different than any other coworker.

What about Randal? Do you feel Tony harnessed any *Relationship Leadership* power abiding by the policy and not trying to give him more punishment than he deserved? Of course, he did. Everyone knows they had disagreements in the past, but Tony was still fair.

Now let's look at this a different way. If you are a parent, you can relate and if not, maybe you will be some day. Do you ever wonder why your three year old intentionally does something you tell him/her not to? Do you think your child simply wants to get in trouble? No, of course not. What your child is doing is testing to see if you have the courage to discipline him/her. If you follow through with the unpleasantness of discipline, it reassures your child that you are strong enough to care for him/her and creates a bond of security and trust.

By disciplining Elizabeth as the policy stated and not letting his fondness for her intervene, Tony was perceived as being able to do the tough thing when it was unpleasant. As for Randal, Tony handled it the same way. He didn't let his dislike for him intervene and Tony was regarded as being fair. Although neither one of them violated policy just to see what Tony would do, his ability to *neutralize his emotions* (both good and bad) toward each of them was seen by everyone that he is strong enough to be their leader. This is the same concept as dealing with the disobedient three year old.

As for Chad, he was not able to neutralize his emotions (both good and bad) when dealing with Rebecca and Priscilla. He let Rebecca off without any discipline and tried to terminate Priscilla. Do you feel anyone trusts they will be fairly disciplined by Chad? I don't!

Do you remember in Chapter 12 (*The First Dance*) how Tony danced with everyone the same? Even when coworkers he recently disciplined asked him to dance, Tony danced with as much enthusiasm as he did everyone else. Now let's equate this to how Tony handled coworkers he liked and disliked when it came to discipline (*The Second Dance*). Again, he neutralized his emotions and treated Elizabeth and Randal the same.

What about Chad in Chapter 12 (*The First Dance*)? Was he equal with his enthusiasm when dancing with someone other than Rebecca? No, and everyone saw it. What about disciplining coworkers he liked and disliked (*The Second Dance*)? Did Chad neutralize his emotions and treat Rebecca and Priscilla the same? No, he did not, and everyone saw it. In other words, Chad doesn't have a clue how to dance with everyone equally!

What I need you to understand is that in a position of Leadership, whether it's *The First Dance* or *The Second Dance*, YOU always dance the same with everyone!

Relationship Leadership Power Harnessed
- Trust
- Ethical
- Fairness
- Firmness
- Respect
- Integrity

Take-Away
Be like Tony and *Don't be like Chad!*

The Principle of Camaraderie

Will you follow someone that you have no bond with and don't like?

Chapter 17

Bridges of Commonality

"Personal relationships are the fertile soil from which all advancement, all success, all achievement in real life grows."

-**Ben Stein**

Today is the first day of work for Sarah at the Woo-Woo factory. Monica (Human Resources Director) is giving her the new employee tour, which includes introduction to the supervisors Tony and Chad.

Chad is aware of the scheduled time for the introduction, but he is thirsty. He leaves his office right before their arrival and heads for the break room to grab a soda. While on his way he passes Monica and Sarah in the hall. Monica stops Chad and introduces him to Sarah. Chad quickly and curtly says, "I'm Chad." He then abruptly walks away without any more conversation, thinking to himself that he did not have time for new employees because he was thirsty and wanted a soda.

Monica knocks on Tony's door and asks if he is busy. Tony immediately stops what he's doing and says, "No, it can wait. Come in and have a seat." She says, "Tony, I want to introduce you to our new employee Sarah."

"Pleasure to meet you Sarah," Tony says as he firmly shakes her hand and looks her square in the eyes.

Tony then asks Sarah if she is local or recently moved to the area. She says, "I'm from Newton County, just east of here." "Awesome! My Grandfather is from there. Do you know any of the Carlton family? My Grandfather's childhood friend was Bill Carlton," inquires Tony. Monica smiles big and says to Tony, "That was my grandfather!" "No way, I met him when I was about 10 years old. He used to go fishing with my grandfather," says Tony. "Was your Grandfather Charles Williams?" asks Sarah. Tony smiles big and says, "Yes, he was."

Tony and Sarah continued the conversation for several minutes. During the conversation Tony learned that he had quite a bit in common with Sarah. Tony learned that she had an eight-year-old daughter that was going to play softball on the same team as his daughter this summer. Tony was in the military at the same time Sarah's husband was, and in the same branch of service. They both liked red wine, both had been married the same amount of time, and one of Sarah's hobbies was scrapbooking her children's sports. Tony's wife also scrapbooked!

After several minutes of talking with Sarah (building *Bridges of Commonality*), Tony tells her that he must get back to work. "It was a pleasure meeting you and I look forward to working together. Welcome aboard," says Tony. Monica replies, "The pleasure was mine and I look forward to working with you too."

A few minutes later Tony walks into Chad's office and asks if he met Sarah, the new employee? Chad says, "Yeah." "What do you think about her?" asks Tony. "I don't know anything about her, so I don't know what to think. If she does her job and is a reliable employee, I do not really care beyond that," says Chad. Tony enthusiastically tells Chad, "I'm looking forward to working with her. She is friendly and we have a lot in common. Our Grandfathers were childhood friends, her husband was in the same branch of the military that I was, she likes red wine, her daughter is going to play on the same softball team as my daughter this summer, and she scrapbooks just like my wife does." Chad abruptly spins his chair away from Tony and toward his computer as he mumbles, "Yeah, whatever."

Summary

Now, ask yourself which one is going to have the best Relationship with Sarah? Obviously, Tony will! Why? Because he took the time to learn a few things he had in common with Sarah. This immediately built a Relationship between the two that will flourish because Sarah now knows she has things in common with her boss. They are now bonded because Tony took the time to build several *Bridges of Commonality*. Going forward, Sarah will feel extremely comfortable working with Tony and learning more about their undiscovered common bonds. In other words, Sarah will also look to build *Bridges of Commonality* with Tony.

Did you get a tour and introductions your first day on the job? Did you find it intimidating to meet new people, especially your boss? Think about the difference between

Tony and Chad's behavior toward Sarah. Was Sarah intimidated by Tony? No, of course not. Was she intimidated by Chad? Yes, he was a total ass, and his behavior was very polarizing!

Building *Bridges of Commonality* is not that difficult and can be mastered with a little bit of practice. All you have to do beyond being polite and open with your demeanor, is to simply ask questions. Most people will answer without hesitation because they *want* to tell you about themselves. They *want* to belong and the quicker the better. Just look at social media. This gives everyone a global platform to tell the world about themselves and a place to belong, and so many do!

When asking questions, do not rapid fire them and do not make it seem like an inquisition. The conversation needs to flow and can be a little tricky with the type of questions you ask. DO NOT be invasive by asking very personal questions. Every workplace has its boundaries for sensitivity. If you are in Leadership, you should know your organization's boundaries.

Look for nuggets in the conversation to build on. I find a lot of success asking about the other person's last name. If I can relate it to someone I know with the same last name, I ask if they know them or are by chance related. Also, are they local, where did they go to high school, college, children, family, etc.? These are things most all of us have in common and are willing to share.

So, let me leave you with this, "*Simply ask, and listen.*"

Relationship Leadership **Power Harnessed**
- Respect
- Bonding
- Caring
- Courtesy
- Friendly
- Acceptance

Take-Away
Be like Tony and *Don't be like Chad!*

CHAPTER 18

Do Me a Favor

"Management is about arranging and telling. Leadership is about nurturing and enhancing."

-**Tom Peters**

As Tony parks his truck he notices the engine seems to be running a bit rough. It's time to start the workday so he decides to deal with it later.

While walking across the parking lot Tony sees Juan. He walks over and asks Juan if he is still building race car engines on the side and Juan says yes. Tony explains that his car is running rough and asks Juan if he has time after work to do him a favor and look at it. Juan quickly says, "Sure thing boss! I can fix it."

What you need to know here is that Tony was a mechanic before he started working at the Woo-Woo factory. He's confident the engine has fouled a plug. It's an old truck with high mileage and this happens occasionally.

Later in the day Chad walks into Tony's office and tells him, "Your truck sounded like it was having engine problems when you parked it this morning." Tony says, "Yeah, I know. Juan is going to *Do Me a Favor* and look at it after work." Chad chuckles and says, "I wouldn't let anyone I work with repair my car, favor or not! I always have a professional repair my vehicle." Tony acknowledges Chad's arrogance and thanks him for the input as Chad struts out of his office.

The workday has ended for Tony and as he's walking across the parking lot, he sees Juan standing beside his truck with a toolbox in hand. "I'm ready to fix it boss," Juan cheerfully says. Tony pops the latch and Juan raises the hood. He asks Tony to start the engine so he can see and hear it run. "I think you have a fouled plug," says Juan. He gets out some tools and removes the spark plug. Then, Juan cleans the plug and sets the gap before putting it back in the engine. "Now give it a start," says Juan. Tony starts the engine, and it is running great. Tony thanks Juan for repairing his truck and Juan replies with, "No worries. I'm glad I could help!"

A few days later Juan is done for the day and walking across the parking lot when he sees Chad trying to get his car started. He stops to offer his help and Chad says, "No thanks, I have a tow truck coming to take it to the dealership." Juan continues by telling Chad that it sounds like a coil wire might be loose and it will only take a minute to repair. Juan says that he fixed Tony's truck a few days ago and he will gladly help Chad if he will let him. "No thanks, I don't need any favors," snips Chad. Disappointed, Juan says okay and leaves. An hour later the tow truck arrives.

Do Me a Favor

Three days later Chad asks Tony if he can take him after work to pick up his car. "Sure," says Tony. He then asks Chad what was wrong with it and Chad says the coil wire was loose. Tony chuckles and says, "Juan could have repaired that for you." Chad sneers at Tony and says, "Yeah, I just need a ride if that's okay with you."

It's Monday morning and Tony is ready to get the work week started. He pushes the start button on his computer and it's not responding properly. Sometimes when the cleaning crew comes in over the weekend, they turn off computers. Because they don't have the password, they aren't able to shut the computer down properly. Simply pressing the power button can cause problems and it seems this is the case.

What you need to know here is that aside from being a former mechanic, Tony took several computer sciences courses in college. He strongly suspects there is a fragmented file that needs to be repaired.

Tony has the floor supervisor send Monty to his office. He knows that Monty is a computer whiz and has a passion for anything tech related. Monty walks in and says, "You need to see me boss?" Tony asks him if he still has the side hustle building and selling computers and Monty says yes. "Can you *Do Me a Favor* and look at my computer? It is not acting right," says Tony. Monty enthusiastically replies, "Sure thing." After about ten minutes Monty tells Tony he found a fragmented file and it was an easy fix. Tony thanks him for his effort and Monty replies, "Anytime, glad to help."

Chad sees Monty walking out of Tony's office and he steps in to inquire about the visit. "What was that about?" asks Chad. Tony tells him that his computer was on the blink, and he asked Monty to do him a favor and look at it. "He had me up and running in ten minutes," says Tony. "Ha! That's what we have an IT department for," barks Chad. Tony acknowledges Chad's arrogance and explains he knew it was a quick fix and this gave Monty an opportunity to do him a favor. Chad quickly replies with, "I don't need any favors from anyone I work with."

Well, a few weeks later it's Monday morning. Chad starts his computer and guess what? Yep, you guessed it! The cleaning crew turned off his computer over the weekend and now it's not working properly. Chad calls the IT department and puts in a repair order. It is two days before IT can get to the work order. Without a computer Chad is a ship adrift in the ocean with no sail. In other words, Chad is very limited with the amount of work he can do because he has no computer.

Two days later Tony notices the IT guy leaving Chad's office. He walks in and inquires why Chad needed IT. Chad tells Tony that when he started his computer on Monday it didn't work properly. He then frustratingly says, "I was down for two days over a fragmented file. It only took them five minutes to repair it." Tony chuckles and explains that he recently had the same problem. However, rather than call IT, Monty did him a favor and repaired it in no time. Chad spins his chair to face his computer monitor and then turns his head toward Tony and stares. Tony grins and Chad says, "Yeah, whatever."

Summary

Before we get started breaking this down understand that if your company has policies in place for in-house experts (IT, machine repair, etc.) to make repairs then follow company policy. This Chapter isn't about finding ways around company policy; it's about using *Relationship Leadership* by asking for a favor.

Do you feel Chad harnessed any *Relationship Leadership* power by refusing Juan's help with his car? I don't! Juan was eager to help and very capable of solving Chad's problem. Instead, Chad denied Juan the opportunity to feel good about himself by lending a helping hand.

What about Chad's computer being down? Everyone knew Chad was without a computer for two days. And, everyone knew (because they talk) Monty had Tony's computer up and running in ten minutes from what turned out to be the same problem Chad had. Do you feel Chad harnessed any *Relationship Leadership* power by not asking Monty to look at his computer? No, he didn't.

Let's look at Tony's truck issue. Do you feel he harnessed any *Relationship Leadership* power by asking Juan to fix it for him? Yes, he did. Although Tony knew what the problem was, he also knew that working on engines was a passion of Juan's. By asking Juan to help, it gave Juan the opportunity to feel good about himself by helping Tony with his problem.

What about Tony's computer issue? Do you feel he harnessed any *Relationship Leadership* power by asking Monty to fix it for him? Again, yes! Tony used the same principle of asking for a favor from Monty that he did with Juan. Monty was given the opportunity to feel good about himself by lending a helping hand.

Let's dig a little bit deeper. When you are in a Leadership role you are perceived to be the expert. Whether you are or not, your coworkers come to you for information and guidance. When Tony asked Juan and Monty for a favor, he reversed the role. Tony became the one in need and they both were given the opportunity to show their expertise over Tony. Yes, Tony knew what the problem was, but he put his coworkers in a position of being able to feel good about themselves by lending a helping hand. Don't let this bonding opportunity pass you by.

In his book *High Performance Habits*, Brendon Burchard writes about the power of asking to do you a favor, "If someone does say yes to helping you, they tend to like you even *more* after they've done something for you. People don't grudgingly help you. If they didn't want to, they'd probably say no. It's counterintuitive, but if getting people to like you *more* is the goal, then just ask them to do you a favor."[1]

So, do ME a favor! When the opportunity presents itself, ask a coworker to do YOU a favor!

***Relationship Leadership* Power Harnessed**
- Trust
- Respect
- Bonding
- Confidence
- Empowerment
- Humility

Take-Away
Be like Tony and *Don't be like Chad!*

Chapter 19

I'm in if You're In

"Leadership is the art of giving people a platform for spreading ideas that work."

-Seth Godin

Knock, knock! Chad responds with, "Come in." Billy walks in and asks Chad if he has a minute to discuss an idea. Chad spins his chair around toward Billy and says, "Sure, go ahead." Billy explains that he wants to try an idea he came up with pertaining to how they stack the pallets of packaged product waiting for shipping. "What is it?" asks Chad. Billy tells him about a new stacking configuration he came up with and wants permission to explore the possibility. Chad abruptly says, "No, it won't work. Anything else I can help you with?" Disappointed, Billy says no and heads back to work.

Later that day at the lunch table, Billy is talking with his coworkers about his interaction with Chad. "Man, Chad is such an Ass!" says Billy. "How so?" asks Amanda. Billy explains how he went to Chad for permission to try his idea about pallet configuration and Chad immediately shut him down. "You should go talk to Tony and see if he will let you try. After all, he is our boss too," says Wanda. Everyone at the lunch table agrees that Billy has a great idea, and he decides to go see Tony.

Relationship Leadership

Knock, knock! "Come in," says Tony. Billy enters and asks for a minute of Tony's time to discuss his idea of pallet configuration. Additionally, he tells Tony that he recently asked Chad for permission and was immediately shut down. After asking Billy some detailed questions Tony says, "Go for it, *I'm in if You're In.*" He asks Billy how long it will take, and Billy says he should be done by 4:00 p.m. "Great! I'll come to the production floor at 4:00 p.m. to see how it's going," says Tony. With a strong expression of excitement Billy thanks Tony for the opportunity.

What you need to understand here is that Tony knows Billy's idea won't work. He tried it a few years ago.

It's 4:00 p.m. and Tony makes his way to the production floor to see how things are going. "How's it going?" Tony asks Billy. "Not good," he says. Billy explains several problems he discovered while working through the configuration idea. Clearly disgusted, Billy says, "I just don't think it will work." After a little more discussion Tony thanks Billy for bringing the idea to him and expresses his appreciation for Billy recognizing a possible opportunity for the company to improve. In turn, Billy thanks Tony for letting him try his idea.

A few days later there is a knock at Chad's door. "Come in," says Chad. It's Gretchen and she wants to discuss an idea she has for reducing the amount of waste when cutting the boxes for packaging. Chad sighs and says, "Okay, let me hear it." Gretchen explains that if they change the angle of the blade on the machine that cuts the cardboard, she believes it will reduce the amount of scrap pieces. This will provide some overlapping and increase

I'm in if You're In

package strength. Chad quickly responds with, "Nope, won't work, can't do it." As Gretchen stares in disbelief Chad asks her if there is anything else she needs from him and she says no. Gretchen is clearly disappointed.

Well, it's lunch time and guess who is the topic of conversation at the lunch table? Yep, you guessed it.....Chad! Gretchen is pissed and ranting about how Chad treated her. "He barely listened, didn't ask me any questions, and then immediately told me it won't work," snaps Gretchen. Paul speaks up and says, "We could have told you how asking Chad for permission to try an idea was going to go. Billy had the same problem a few days ago." Tammy tells Gretchen that she should take her idea to Tony because that is what Billy did. "Even though it didn't work, Tony gave him permission to try," says Tammy. Everyone agrees and encourages Gretchen to take her idea to Tony. She agrees to do so after lunch.

Knock, knock! "Come in," says Tony. Gretchen enters and asks for a minute of Tony's time to discuss an idea she has. Tony says, "Sure, let's hear it." Gretchen explains that if they change the angle of the blade on the machine that cuts the cardboard, she believes it will reduce the amount of scrap pieces. This will provide some overlapping and increase package strength. After asking some questions, Tony responds with, "Sounds like a great idea. *I'm in if You're In!* When do you want to do it?" Gretchen tells Tony that she can have the cutting machine adjusted and begin testing in about an hour. Tony acknowledges the one-hour time and tells Gretchen to let him know if she needs any help.

Now what you need to know here is that Tony has no clue if Gretchen's idea will work. No one has ever presented this idea to Leadership and he's curious to see if Gretchen can make it work.

About an hour later Tony makes his way to the production floor. He walks up to Gretchen and asks her "Well, how's it going?" Riddled with excitement Gretchen yells, "It worked!" Tony congratulates her on the accomplishment and thanks Gretchen for bringing the idea to his attention. In turn, she thanks him for allowing her to test the idea.

The workday is almost over, and Chad can't let it go. He heard the good news about the success of Gretchen's idea and walks into Tony's office unannounced. He wants to know why Tony is letting coworkers try their ideas. Tony responds with, "Why wouldn't I?" Chad sharply answers with, "They aren't paid to come up with ideas, they are paid to work. Finding better methods of production is our job." Tony thinks for a few seconds, smiles really big, and then says, "Well, although Billy's idea didn't work, Gretchen's did! If it's your job, why didn't you come up with the same idea before she did?" Obviously pissed, Chad scoffs and stomps out of Tony's office while barking his usual response, "Yeah, whatever."

Summary

Could Chad have been any more arrogant? Do you feel he harnessed any *Relationship Leadership* power by denying Billy's request to test his idea? No, he didn't. What about the disappointment Billy felt? Did Chad harness any *Relationship Leadership* power by harshly disappointing Billy? No, of course not.

What about Gretchen? Did Chad harness any *Relationship Leadership* power by treating her the same way he did Billy? No, he didn't. Chad quickly told Gretchen that her idea will not work. He did so with little discussion and never explored the possibility that it might work.

How much *Relationship Leadership* power do you think Tony harnessed when he listened to Billy and asked him to further explain his idea? Even though Tony knew it wouldn't work, he didn't shut Billy's idea down and make him feel inferior. Instead, Tony asked Billy for more information which gave him the opportunity to work through the idea and basically sell it to Tony. Even in the wake of failure, by allowing Billy to do this and then try the idea, it bolstered his self-confidence. Did this also harness any *Relationship Leadership* power for Tony?

Let's look at how Tony handled Gretchen. Did he harness any *Relationship Leadership* power? Yes, of course he did. Tony treated Gretchen's idea the same as Billy's and treated her with the same respect as Billy. The bonus here is that Gretchen's idea worked.

We can't forget the lunch table crew. Did Tony harness any *Relationship Leadership* power with them? Yes, he did! As you have learned by now, *they talk.* Everyone was aware of Tony allowing Billy and Gretchen to try their ideas and Chad refusing. How much *Relationship Leadership* power do you feel Chad harnessed from the lunch table crew? How about zero!

As a leader you should always listen to your coworker's ideas, concerns, and suggestions. Whether you know the solution or not, treat it the same every time. If there is no potential physical or emotional harm in allowing something that you know will fail, let it happen. This is a great opportunity for coworkers to learn, grow, and build self-confidence. By agreeing to this (*I'm in if You're In*) you share ownership of the failure or success. You harness *Relationship Leadership* power either way!

Relationship Leadership Power Harnessed
- Trust
- Respect
- Supportive
- Equality
- Dignity
- Confidence

Take-Away
Be like Tony and *Don't be like Chad!*

CHAPTER 20

Power of a Nickname

"Words have meaning and names have power."

-Author Unknown

Lynne is in Tony's office having a general conversation when she notices a framed photo. She asks, "Is that the 7th hole at Pebble beach?" Tony responds, "Yes, I played a round there several years ago." Lynne tells Tony that she is a golfer and loves to play. They talk a bit more about the game and Tony says, "We should play a round sometime." Lynne agrees and says, "What about Sunday at 12:00 p.m.? I have a tee time reserved." Tony quickly says, "I would love to." They agree that Sunday it is!

Sunday rolls around and Lynne tees up on the first hole. She smacks a long drive straight down the middle of the fairway and Tony says, "Nice shot." Tony tees up and slices his ball a little to the right. "Oh well, at least it's still in the fairway," chuckles Tony.

As they work their way toward the 18th hole, Tony notices that Lynne is a particularly good golfer. She is two strokes under par and only three holes left. What Tony does not know is that Lynne was a collegiate scholarship golfer.

The 18th hole is a par 5 and Lynne makes the green in three strokes. However, she is at the edge of the green and about twenty-five feet from the hole. Tony says, "This is going to be a tough putt, maybe you can get close enough for a second putt and par the hole." Lynne grins and says, "Oh yeah, watch this." She takes steady aim and gently putts the ball. Tony cannot believe what he is seeing. The ball is heading straight for the hole, drops in. Tony is riddled with excitement and says, "That was one hell of a putt! You birdied the hole!" Then Lynne informs Tony that she played college golf. He laughs and jokingly accuses her of suckering him into an ass kicking. Tony tells Lynne because that was such a memorable putt, "I'm going to call you *Putter*." She smiles and says, "Putter, huh? Yeah, I like it."

As they are walking back to the golf cart Tony is limping. When he goes to sit in the cart he winces and grabs his knee. Lynne sees this and asks him if something is wrong. Tony replies, "It's no big deal, I'm just getting old." Lynne asks, "Well, how old are you?" Tony thinks for a second and responds with, "Let's just say I'm the last of the Baby-Boomer generation." She chuckles and says, "That's it, I'm going to call you *Boomer*." Tony laughs and says, "Okay Putter, you can call me Boomer."

It is Monday morning and Tony and Chad pass Lynne as they are walking to their offices. She smiles and says, "How's it going Boomer?" Tony quickly responds, "What's up Putter?" Chad is confused but does not say anything.

Later that day everyone is enjoying their break when the cafeteria door opens and in walks Chad. Paul sees Chad

Power of a Nickname

and says, "Don't look now, but Captain Asshat just walked in." Everyone chuckles and Diane asks Paul why he calls Chad Captain Asshat. He responds with, "Well, he definitely makes the effort to ensure everyone knows he is in charge, so that makes him the Captain. And, the way he treats everyone makes him an Asshat. So, I call him Captain Asshat!" The table erupts with laughter and then Mitch says, "I call him Mirror Man." Curious, Teresa asks Mitch to explain. He says, "Every time he walks by a mirror Chad stops to look at himself." Again, the table erupts with laughter and then Paula chimes in, "I call him Mr. Personality." When asked for an explanation she tells everyone, "Because he has no personality."

It's almost quitting time when Chad walks into Tony's office and says, "Curiosity has the best of me, who's Putter and Boomer?" Tony tells Chad about their golf game and the memorable putt Lynne made. He went on to explain how he captured the moment by giving her the nickname Putter. Then, Tony explains how Lynne gave him the nickname Boomer. With his usual disenchanting commentary Chad replies, "Why would you do that? I only call people by their given name." Tony takes a few minutes and explains the *Power of a Nickname* principal to Chad. Not surprisingly, Chad shakes his head left to right and mutters, "Yeah, whatever."

Summary

In this scenario Chad did not have the opportunity to harness any *Relationship Leadership* power by using a nickname. He did, however, present Tony with a negative position of this *Relationship Leadership* principle.

Do you feel Tony harnessed any *Relationship Leadership* power by giving Lynne the nickname Putter? Yes, he did! Tony understands the *Power of a Nickname* principle and how to use it. Regardless of who calls her Putter, when Lynne hears it, she will always think of the day she made that twenty-five-foot putt.

Let us explore this a little further. Nicknames are widely used in our culture and have been since the dawn of mankind. Think about it. From athletes to celebrities, politicians, criminals, military, family members, friends, etc., a nickname is used as frequently as a given name. The more a nickname spreads, the fewer people know its true meaning and history. Therefore, you have a responsibility to effectively use the *Power of a Nickname* principle.

The most important part of this principle is to only give someone a nickname when it can be linked to a positive event. Nicknames are a powerful double-sided coin; In that you can just as easily create a negative nickname for someone by linking it to an unpleasant event. If you choose to give someone a nickname, make sure they are receptive, and the connotation is positive!

Once the negative nickname calling begins, everyone wants to be in the club. Look at how Chad's coworkers tagged him with negative nicknames. As soon as Paul called Chad Captain Asshat, several more nicknames surfaced and none of them were positive. Rather than look for the opportunity to give Chad a positive nickname, they all focused on sharing their negative ones. This is a position you do not want to be in with your coworkers. If you effectively practice *Relationship Leadership* Principles, you won't be.

Do you have a nickname? I bet you do, and I bet you can tell me in detail when and how you came by it. I have accumulated several over the years and I can tell you the history of each one. The strongest nickname I have is the one I use as the author of this book.....Eddie Mac.

One more thing I need you to clearly understand. DO NOT randomly give EVERY coworker a nickname. If you do, you will look like an idiot and your use of the *Power of a Nickname* principle will backfire.

Think about it this way; The *Power of a Nickname* principle is social currency. Make sure you spend thriftly, and do not make any bad purchases!

***Relationship Leadership* Power Harnessed**
- Respect
- Bonding
- Identity
- Acceptance
- Recognition
- Camaraderie

Take-Away
Be like Tony and *Don't be like Chad!*

Chapter 21

Bump It

"Earn your leadership every day."

-Michael Jordan

It is total chaos at the Woo-Woo factory! As soon as the production line was powered up to start the day's work, everything immediately shut down. Nothing is working and has not for about an hour. No one knows what the problem is, and everyone is in fear of being sent home and losing a day of pay.

Tony is on the production floor helping maintenance run diagnostic tests. Chad, well, Chad is being an awesome spectator. It is Chad's position that he is in Leadership and not maintenance. Therefore, it is not his job to be tinkering with the equipment and troubleshooting. Tony, well, he has a different view. He feels it his role as a member of Leadership to help any way he can.

After quite some time of troubleshooting to no avail, Rod looks at Tony and says, "I have an idea." He explains to Tony that he suspects one of the microprocessors is bad and thinks he knows which one. The only way to test his theory is to bypass the bad microprocessor. There are enough microprocessors to compensate for the bypass and if it works the production line will start. However, this is a short-term fix because this will eventually cause all microprocessors to fail. If it works, production will be operational for about 48 hours before failure. Tony tells Rod that before he runs the bypass let him check if he can get a microprocessor shipped within 48 hours.

About 20 minutes later Tony returns and tells Rod that he can have a replacement microprocessor within 24 hours. With the plan of action in place, Tony kills the power to the production line and Rod begins wiring. 30 minutes later Rod says, "Bypass is done and I'm ready, boss."

Tony turns on the power and the production line powers up as if nothing went wrong. The place erupts with cheers and clapping for Rod. No one is going to lose a day of pay! Tony walks over to Rod, congratulates him, and extends a fist. Rod smiles, makes a fist, and bumps Tony's fist. Chad sees the fist bump, rolls his eyes, and returns to his office without congratulating Rod.

A few days later Tony and Chad are in the hallway talking when Arlene walks up. She tells them she just learned that Simone is turning 50 in a few days. Arlene wants to know if she can have a surprise birthday party at lunchtime on Friday. She plans on decorating the cafeteria and inviting Simone's family. Tony says, "That's a great idea! Can I bring the cake?" Simone says, "Absolutely!" Tony then says, "It's a deal, I'm bringing the cake and you're taking care of the rest." He then extends a fist and Arlene bumps Tony's fist with hers and says, "Deal!" Again, Chad rolls his eyes and walks off.

Knock, knock! It is Chad and he wants to talk. Chad enters and immediately asks Tony, "What's up with all the fist bumping?" Tony responds with, "What do you mean?" Chad tells Tony, "It seems like every time someone accomplishes something, or you make an agreement, you give them a fist bump." Chad continues with, "I think it's ridiculous. I don't touch other people, and especially when they are just doing their job." Tony sighs and then explains to Chad the *Relationship Leadership* principle of *Bump It.* After listening to Tony's explanation, Chad turns to walk away and then stops and says, "Yeah, whatever."

Summary

By now you have probably figured out that Chad is simply not going to change, and obviously is not willing to embrace any *Relationship Leadership* principles. Right?

Do you feel Chad harnessed any *Relationship Leadership* power when he did not congratulate Rod, rolled his eyes at the fist bump, and walked away? No, of course not! What about not offering to help with Simone's party, rolling his eyes at the fist bump, and walking away? Again, no!

What about Tony? Did he harness any *Relationship Leadership* power when he congratulated Rod with a fist bump in front of the whole workforce? Yes, of course he did! And, when Tony offered to help Arlene with Simone's birthday party, did he harness any *Relationship Leadership* power by sealing the deal with a fist bump? Again, yes! Tony understands the *Bump It Relationship Leadership* principle and how to use it. He knows that when effectively used, the fist bump builds unity.

When we look at where we are today as a society and its accepted norms, the sand has shifted. With the onset of COVID-19, handshaking is far less acceptable than it used to be. Also, many people are now averse to being touched without solicitation. In other words, randomly putting your hand on someone's shoulder, hugging them, or being overly affectionate is simply not as accepted as it used to be. Tony knows this and therefore he avoids the possibility of upsetting someone by offering them a fist bump. In turn, they are acknowledging the approval or agreement, and choosing to participate in being touched.

Now, DO NOT constantly fist bump everyone for every little thing! If you do, you will look like an idiot and devalue this *Relationship Leadership* principle. You need to create value with a fist bump by reserving it for times of approval or agreement.

What I need you to understand is that just like in the last chapter, the *Bump It Relationship Leadership* principle is social currency. Again, spend thriftly, and do not make any bad purchases!

Relationship Leadership Power Harnessed
- Unity
- Camaraderie
- Bonding
- Acceptance
- Agreement
- Respect

Take-Away
Be like Tony and *Don't be like Chad!*

Bonus

Digital Dilemma

"The truth is we will be forever haunted by traceable communications manifested in the digital world."

-Germany Kent

This chapter does not involve any scenarios with Tony and Chad and is not a *Relationship Leadership* principle. However, before you venture into the Leadership arena with the principles you learned, I strongly feel we need to have a short discussion. You know, just you and me.

Have you ever stopped and thought about how much we use digital communication? Well, I have, and it is mind boggling. Yes, we live in a digital age, and I get it! My question is do you?

How many times a day do you text, email, or post on social media? With the number of social media platforms available it is easy to post on one and your message(s) simultaneously posts on several others. Also, if you post something and it goes viral, well, then you have really extended your exposure.

What does this mean? If you do not clearly understand your impact as a leader when using digital media, Leadership failure just might be in your future. You see, everything you put out in digital form is an extension of your Leadership. This means when you are off work too. If your coworkers see you as a great leader at work and see a totally different person on social media, you are doomed as a leader. In a Leadership role everyone is always watching, and remember, they talk. So, I cannot stress enough that the leader you are in person and the person you are on social media must be one in the same. There is no room for difference here. To be a great leader (and I know you will), you must hold yourself to a high standard of behavior. Be consistent and always conduct yourself as if everyone is watching, because they probably are. So, I am challenging you to ask yourself this question each time before you post on social media. *Will my coworkers approve of this post as their leader?*

Now, on to texting and email. These are informal forms of communication that need to be handled with care. It is easy to become passive aggressive when sending text/email (we discussed this when Chad sent an email about improper employee parking). Be mindful of this and I challenge you to always read your text/email two or three times before sending. Try to read your message from the perspective of the person receiving it. If you cannot seem to find the right words for the desired meaning, contact them in person instead. Think about it. Have you ever received a message/email, got pissed, and then discovered when you spoke in person that the message/email did not have the meaning you thought? Or have you sent a message/email only to find out the person misinterpreted the meaning? Well, let me tell you, I have....and I still have the scars to prove it.

Do you realize that every digital communication is recorded? Social media/text messages/email are handled by data centers or in-house servers. The "cloud" is a data center that records everything! How do you think scandalous messages/posts find their way into the headlines years after they were supposedly "deleted?" Understand there is always a record of your activity and, as a leader, I expect you to conduct yourself accordingly.

Last but certainly not least. Did you know that if your employer provides you a cell phone and/or email all communication that you generate may not be as private as you think? Now I am not an attorney, but I am confident that most states (and the Government) view the digital communication exchanged on a platform/device the employer provides (pays for) as property of the employer. Depending on the circumstance(s) this means that your social media posts can be scrutinized as well. In other words, if your employer conducts an internal investigation or they end up in a lawsuit involving digital communication that you generated with their platform/device, do not expect any privacy.

Take-Away.
Do not let digital communication become a dilemma!

Final Words

"Leadership is a journey. Each one of us has to take our own path, and get there our own way."

-David Gergen

Well, you did it! You made it through the most simple and powerful book on Leadership that you will ever read. Not only did you just make it through, but you also learned how to harness the power of leading with Relationships!

As you grow in your Leadership career, I hope you embrace the principles you learned and refer to this book often. Understand that to be a great leader, you must always be learning and taking the next step toward Leadership development. Everyone's path is different, and it will not always be easy. Stay the course and you will eventually make it to the top of your Leadership game.

Think of it like this. Do you know someone that is a great leader? If so, have you ever wondered how they attained their Leadership capabilities? Well, let me help you with a few word pictures that might bring this into focus.

Imagine that because of their Leadership ability their Leadership plane flies at an altitude of 30,000 feet. Now you know as well as I do that a plane does not magically start flying at 30,000 feet. So, how did they get to that Leadership altitude? They started by boarding their Leadership plane, buckling in, setting a course, taxiing to the runway, and then taking off. Once they began flying, their Leadership plane slowly *ascended* to 30,000 feet. During this time, their Leadership plane was not level, there was turbulence along the way, and the pilot's seat was uncomfortable at times.

Because of your commitment to learn and practice *Relationship Leadership* principles, you have already boarded your Leadership plane, and are ready for takeoff. Although there will be turbulence along the way, and the pilot's seat may get uncomfortable at times, how high your Leadership plane flies and where it goes is up to YOU!

...Successful travels, my friend!

About Eddie Mac

Born in Western Kentucky, Eddie Mac grew up in a low income and mixed-race neighborhood. He has often said that he would not trade it for any other experience.

Eddie Mac was first exposed to Leadership while playing high school football. He witnessed fellow players and coaches lead their team to a State Championship title. As an athlete, he was held to a higher standard on and off the field. Along with this Integrity, Eddie Mac learned about Communication, Respect, and Camaraderie. As he saw the athlete brotherhood develop, strengthen, and ultimately become a team of champions, Eddie Mac knew the impact would be with him for the rest of his life.

After high school, Eddie Mac attended college before entering a career in law enforcement. During his 20 years of service, Eddie Mac earned the rank of Administrative Captain and completed several hundred hours of advanced Leadership and executive development training. He was a S.W.A.T. Commander, Shift Commander, and Administrator of other specialty units. These included Bomb Squad, D.A.R.E., and Field Training.

As his law enforcement career ended, Eddie Mac felt his Leadership knowledge had culminated to the point that he could help others with their Leadership journey. After several more years of research and education, Eddie Mac decided it was time to develop a Leadership model that is simple and powerful. With his focus on new leaders, and the goal of being easy to understand and repeatedly used, *Relationship Leadership* was born.

I Need Your Help!

"Those who are happiest are those who do the most for others."

-Booker T. Washington

The way this works is that for Relationship Leadership to reach as many new leaders as possible, positive online reviews are necessary. The more received, the higher-ranking Relationship Leadership will achieve. Hence, more new leaders will see the benefits of Relationship Leadership based on what you tell them!

I have confidence in Relationship Leadership, and I have confidence in you. So many new leaders have no clue where to start their Leadership journey. This is your opportunity to help them "set their cornerstone." Please, go online *right now* and leave a positive review.

Simply put, they need your help, and *I Need Your Help!*

Training

"Development is a cornerstone for Leadership."

- Eddie Mac

What does the Leadership training platform look like at your place of employment?
- Are all new leaders given the same training to begin their Leadership journey?
- Is everyone given the same opportunity to succeed?
- Is a structured Leadership succession plan in place?

If none of these exist, why don't they? Now that you are in Leadership, ask your boss about the next steps for your journey. If the answers are not clear, I can help!

At Relationship Leadership Training, I offer Leadership development planning, succession planning, consulting, coaching, public speaking, in-person training, and online training. To learn more, visit me online or contact me.

RelationshipLeadership.net

Suggested Next Reads

Psychogeometrics
-Susan Delinger

How to Win Friends and Influence People
-Dale Carnegie

Emotional Intelligence 2.0
-Travis Bradberry
-Jean Greaves

Who Moved My Cheese?
-Spencer Johnson, M.D.

Suggested Next Level Reads

Extreme Ownership
-Jocko Willink

The 7 Habits Of Highly Effective People
-Stephen R. Covey

High Performance Habits
-Brendon Burchard

Drive
-Daniel H. Pink

Atomic Habits
-James Clear

Followership: What It Takes to Lead
-James Schindler

Endnotes

Chapter 1 - 100% and 100%

1. Understand that Matrix style is for management and not Leadership. I only used this because I needed a management structure to help illustrate the 100% and 100% principle. Management style(s) are not a focus of this chapter/book. See Stuckenbruck, L. C. (1979).

Chapter 5 - Personalities and Learning

1. ENTJ: MBTI® personality profile. Eu.themyersbriggs.com. (2021).

2. Gallup, I. (2021).

3. At the time of this writing Psychogeometrics was not in print. I spoke with CEO Susan Hite and she shared with me the book is under revision and will be available soon. You can learn more about this personality assessment tool at Psychogeometrics.com. See Dellinger, S. (1989).

4. Dellinger, S. (1989).

Chapter 9 - Less Than Perfect

1. Although Drive is an excellent read, it is about what motivates human beings and not necessarily

Leadership. I used Pink's Mastery Asymptote explanation because it is an excellent fit to help explain the Less Than Perfect principle. Motivation factors as described by Pink are not a focus of this chapter/book. See Pink, D. (2009).

2. Pink, D. (2009).

Chapter 18 – Do Me a Favor

1. Burchard, B. (2017).

References

Dellinger, S. (1989). Psychogeometrics. Prentice-Hall.

ENTJ: MBTI® personality profile. Eu.themyersbriggs.com. (2021). Retrieved 9 March 2021, from https://eu.themyersbriggs.com/en/tools/MBTI/MBTI-personality-Types/ENTJ.

Gallup, I. (2021). How CliftonStrengths Compares With Strengths Profile. Gallup.com. Retrieved 9 March 2021, from https://www.gallup.com/cliftonstrengths/en/249497/compare-strengths-profile Cliftonstrengths .aspx.

Pink, D. (2009). Drive [Kindle Ebook] (p. 124). Riverhead Books.

Stuckenbruck, L. C. (1979). The Matrix Organization. Project Management Quarterly, 10(3), 21-33. Retrieved 8 April 2021, from https://www.pmi.org/ learning/ library /matrix-organization-structurereason-evolution-1837

Burchard, B. (2017). High Performance Habits (p. 224). Hay House, Inc.

Fist Bump - Illustration 1030940986 © Irina Karpinchik | iStockphoto.com